MW00736663

The Study
and Writing
of History

The Study and Writing of History

Gary Hermalyn

THE BRONX COUNTY HISTORICAL SOCIETY

The Study and Writing of History
by Dr. Gary Hermalyn
Copyright © 2007
The Bronx Country Historical Society
All rights reserved. Printed in the United States of America.
No part of this book may be used or reproduced in any manner
whatsoever without written permission except in the case
of brief quotations embodied in critical articles and reviews.

For information contact:
The Bronx Country Historical Society,
3309 Bainbridge Avenue,
The Bronx, NY 10467

www.bronxhistoricalsociety.org

ISBN 0-941-980-50-2

Design and Graphics: Henry C. Meyer, Jr.

Acknowledgements

The author extends his thanks to Frederick M. Binder for his fine course, which illuminated this subject at Columbia University Teachers College, Dr. Peter Derrick, Dr. Elizabeth Beirne, Mr. B. O'Connor Pythagoras, Ms. Kathleen A. McAuley, and Ms. Teresa Moran.

Morris High School, the first New York City
Public High School in The Bronx, opened in 1904.
It served boys and girls and was the first
co-ed school in the city.
It is located on 166th Street between Boston Road
and Jackson Avenue. Postcard view c. 1906.

*The Bronx County Historical Society
Research Library.*

Table of Contents

Illustrations, Maps & Tables

DeWitt Clinton High School for boys
opened in 1906 in Manhattan.
One of the first of three New York City Public
High Schools, it was located on 10th Avenue
between 58th and 59th Streets.
Today, it is the home of John Jay College.
Photo c.1920.
*The Bronx County Historical Society
Research Library.*

Introduction

Most history books deal with a historical place, period, person, or topic. This work deals with the general problems of the historical method of research and writing. To study history and the techniques of the historian is to attempt to understand the world and such study can easily move from the local to the international scene.

But why do we study history? Because history concerns our lives, our time and our ability to make choices.

History is an intellectual discipline and tradition, which enables us to use certain techniques to see relationships and forces at work. History is mostly written between the possible and probable truth.

Lewis and Clark discovered Florida. Is this statement correct?

Is this statement improbable? "Yes." Are there contradictions in documents? Well yes, in this case the evidence is clear that Lewis and Clark were among the first Americans to travel to the Pacific Ocean and not to discover Florida.

So a conclusion is reached when you, the researcher, becomes so confident in your material that no further research is necessary. Keep in mind that there are two kinds of criticism, external and internal. External criticism is the accuracy of a document: does it fit its time and place, is it authentic? While internal criticism is whether the document is credible, can it be true?

Historians must be objective. One must collect information and then do analysis. One cannot always tell what will be an historical event; even those present at the time of the event are not always correct. Future President John Adams, for example, wrote to his wife Abigail that July 2nd would be a historic day of celebration honoring the signing of the Declaration of Independence in the new country. And yet the real day of honor became July 4th.

Another case is President Franklin Roosevelt calling December 7, 1941, when Japan attacked Pearl Harbor, "a day which will live in infamy." This date's meaning is now oftentimes forgotten. So while a historic event, it has lost its distinguishing characteristic. For what can we call September 11, 2001, but a day of infamy and the beginning of the United States' war on terror.

A historian compares evidence and corroborates information, wherever one can. Each problem is unique. One good eyewitness is better than three unreliable, hearsay witnesses. Statistical sources are now readily available for quantitative methods of corroboration on virtually any topic such as population demographics, births and deaths, reading levels, voting records, etc. Through the use of data to confirm a hypothesis, perhaps through a quantitative analysis, one can correct, confirm, or even deny a position.

When looking for historical documentation you must realize that 19th century historians were less critical. To solve such problems, get close to the sources. 21st century writers, on the other hand, are almost too critical. Again the sources are the key.

Seeking fundamental similarities between things that are apparently different gives you a hypothesis. While that original hypothesis may change as contrary elements crop up, you probably will begin to see a direction. But always beware of bias (do not be blind to facts, as this interferes with history by ignoring evidence and uses only material that supports your argument), ethnocentrisms, and oversimplification.

How do we write history?

A) What are historical questions – how are they formulated?

B) What are historical techniques?

C) What are historical sources and how do we locate them?

D) What do we mean by written history?

To explore these questions we will be alternating between theory and practice utilizing different exercises related to historical research and writing. They will provide the reader with a beginning foundation to understand the variations in history writing whether it is for a family history, a history of the Gulf War, the Renaissance, or your neighborhood's story. One needs to start at a specific point and bring forth your arguments in a logical manner to a conclusion backed up by evidence from the various forms of written records, oral traditions, media records, eyewitnesses, etc.

Finally, historians should be impartial and fair. In the search for truth, be open to its results.

Wadleigh High School for girls opened in 1902
in Manhattan and was the first of the three
New York City Public High School buildings.
It was located at 114th-115th Street
between 7th and 8th Avenues.
The Bronx County Historical Society
Research Library.

The Study
and Writing
of History

General George Washington at Trenton,
painting by John Trumbull,1792.

Yale University Art Gallery, New Haven, CT.
Postcard, The Bronx County Historical Society Collection.

1.

Verification of a "Simple Historical Fact"

When was George Washington's birthday?

As you proceed, keep a careful record of each step in your search.

For example, begin by checking George Washington in the dictionary, and then in an encyclopedia or on-line.

When you have found the answer to your satisfaction, write a brief statement in a page or two describing what you found out and include the false steps. Then explain how you know the answer is correct by trying to trace your information to its source.

Entries by an unknown hand in the family Bible
(located at Mount Vernon, Virginia) of the births and deaths
of the children of Augustine and Mary Ball Washington.
The date of George Washington's birth was entered as
February 11, 1731/30 "old style." By the calendar
corrected in 1752, the date was February 22, 1732, "New Style."
Photocopy courtesy of the Mount Vernon Ladies' Association.

VERIFICATION OF A HISTORICAL FACT: WHEN WAS GEORGE WASHINGTON'S BIRTHDAY?

Consulted the following sources to verify Washington's birth date:

1. *The World Almanac 1982* (New York: Newspaper Enterprise Association, 1982), p. 783.

The British Government imposed the Gregorian calendar on all its possessions, including the American colonies, in 1752. The British decreed that the day following September 2, 1752, should be called September 14, a loss of 11 days. All dates preceding were marked O. S., for Old Style. In addition, New Year's Day was moved to January 1st from March 25th (e.g. under the old reckoning, March 24, 1700 had been followed by March 25, 1701). George Washington's birth date, which was February 11, 1731, O. S., became February 22, 1732, N. S. (New Style).

2. Ibid., p. 788.

Here Washington's birthday was listed as a federal legal holiday celebrated on the third Monday in February.

3. *The Encyclopedia of New York City*, (New Haven: Yale University Press, 1995), p.1242, provided the date for Washington's birthday as February 22, 1732, with no mention of Old Style calendar date.

4. *New Columbia Encyclopedia* (New York: Columbia University Press, 1975), p. 2933.

This source confirmed the first, i. e., George Washington's birth date was February 11, 1731 O. S., February 22, 1732 N. S.

5. James T. Flexner, *The Forge of Experience* (1732–1775) Vol. 1 (New York: Little Brown & Co., 1965), p. 12.

In footnote #5 Flexner confirmed birth date as February 11, 1731 O.S., February 22, 1732 N.S.

6. Douglas Southhall Freeman, *George Washington, A Biography. Vol. 1, Young Washington* (New York: Charles Scribner's Sons, 1948), frontispiece, and p. 47.

This biography confirms birth date as above, and provides a reproduction of the record of Washington's birth from the family Bible.

7. Paul Wilstach, *Mount Vernon: Washington's Home and the Nation's Shrine* (Garden City: Doubleday, 1925), p. 250.

An illustration and narrative describing the tomb of Washington indicate that it provides no information concerning the birth (or death) date, but is labeled only "Washington."

8. Ibid., p. 10.

Cites copy of section from family Bible to confirm birth date:

"George Washington son to Augustine and Mary his wife was born on the 11th day of February 1731-32 about 10 in the morning and was baptized the 5th of April . . ."

Note that both years are given, i. e. 1731-32. So clearly this was written after September 2, 1752. This practice was to avoid confusion. (See: *New Columbia Encyclopedia*, op. cit., p. 422)

9. John Fitzpatrick, ed., *Diaries of Washington (1748-1799)*, Vol. IV (1789-1799) (New York: Houghton Mifflin Co., 1925), p. 298.

The entry for February 11, 1799 is:

"Went up to Alexandria to the celebration of my birthday. Many maneuvers were performed by the Uniform Corps, and an elegant Ball and Supper at night."

Note that Wilstach (op. cit.) claimed that Birth Night Balls were given as early as 1784 when General and Mrs. Washington went to Alexandria, Virginia for the first one.

10. Sue Keeler, Mount Vernon Ladies' Association of the Union, telephone interview, September 26, 1982.

Ms. Keeler confirmed that the Washington family Bible that records George's birth date is in the collection at Mount Vernon. It is periodically exhibited in the museum.

11. John Rhodelhamel, Archivist, Mount Vernon Ladies' Association of the Union, telephone interview, September 27, 1982.

Mr. Rhodelhamel felt that the family Bible is the authoritative source for the birth date. He forwarded to the author a copy of the page in the bible. (See illustration.)

Summary

If the Washington family Bible is true, it is the primary source for the birth date of George Washington on February 11, 1731 O. S., February 22, 1732 N. S., yet, this entry was clearly written after 1752. So the best evidence is Washington's diary entry which makes us confident about the day, February 11, but not so the year, as we know Washington made the entry in his own hand.

2.

Researching an Individual

Here is a set of questions about British historian Edward Hallett Carr. Such questions can easily be translated to any individual you are researching.

Who was E. H. Carr?

Did E. H. Carr have a clear point of view? Was he politically active? What did he write about? Was he a controversial historian? These are questions that may help you in your research.

Keep a list of each step you take, in the same manner that you did in the previous exercise. Make a special note of anything you believe might have influenced Carr's interpretation of history.

RESEARCHING AN INDIVIDUAL:
WHO WAS E. H. CARR, THE HISTORIAN?

The following steps were taken to establish
E. H. Carr's identity:

1. Edward Hallett Carr. *What is History?* (New York: Vintage Books, 1962).

The biographical sketch at the back of this book by Carr indicated that he was a British author born in 1892. His professional career included being part of the British delegation at the Peace Conference of 1919. He was later involved with the British Foreign Office and concerned with Russian affairs following the Bolshevik Revolution. He was with the British Foreign Office until 1936 when he became a Professor of International Politics at the University College of Wales (until 1947). From 1941 until 1946 he was an editor of *The Times of London.* In the 1950s, he was part of the academic worlds of Oxford and Cambridge. He was the author of several books on political science, and had a monumental work-in-progress, *A History of Soviet Russia* of which seven volumes appeared from 1950 on.

2. Miranda Herbert and Barbara McNeil eds. *Biography and Genealogy Master Index.* Second Edition, Vol. 2. (Detroit: Gale Research Company, 1980), p. 63.

This indicated biographical sources of information on Carr including *Contemporary Authors* and *Who's Who.*

3. Cynthia Fadool, (ed.). *Contemporary Authors:*
A Bibliographical Guide to Current Author's and Their Works. Vols. 61-64. (Detroit: Gale Research Company, 1976) pp. 105-106.

This provided a detailed account of Carr's life including personal information about his education, home, office, career information with further details on his work with the British Foreign Office, and memberships, awards and honors, such as Commander of the Order of the British Empire.

It lists his writings chronologically and makes clear that his interest was in political history, particularly that of Russia. The comments about Carr said that he was "an Olympian among historians" (A.J.P. Taylor), and that his works were "a welcome antidote to the offering of the university and government mystagogues who have filled so many volumes of nonsense about Russia" (*Virginia Quarterly Review*).

4. *Who's Who 1982-1983: Annual Biographical Dictionary.* (New York: St. Martin's Press, 1982), p. 364.

This source provided a year by year abbreviated list of Carr's education, professional life and writings, most of which were covered in previously consulted sources.

5. *The Times of London Index.* July, 1978-April, 1982.

The references were as follows:

TLS = *Times Literary Supplement.*

ST = *Sunday Times.*

THES = *Times Higher Education Supplement.*

DT = *Daily Times*

Carr, *From Napoleon to Stalin and Other Essays,* (THES) April 10, 1981.

Carr, *The Russian Revolution from Lenin to Stalin,* (TLS) November 23, 1979.

Carr's book choice during TLS absence, (TLS) November 23, 4b (1979).

Carr, *A History of Soviet Russia,* (DT) January 11, 8d. (1979).

Profile: Cartoon, (THES) July 7, 7a; 1 (THES) 14, 27d. (1978).

Carr, *Foundations of a Planned Economy 1926-1929,* (ST) February 13, 40d., (THES) July 15, 20e. (1978).

6. *New York Times Biographical Service,* January, 1977-July, 1982.

New York Times Index January, 1980-March 1982.

New York Times Individual Edition Indexes, April 1982-present.

These sources contained only a few book reviews.

7. C. Abramsky. *Essays in Honor of E. H. Carr.* (Hamden, Conn.: Archon Books, 1974).

This book was written by a group of scholars who presented papers in honor of Carr's eightieth birthday on June 28, 1972. In the "Tribute to E. H. Carr" (pp. vii-viii) it stated that he "alone in Western Europe . . . has achieved a position of pre-eminence primarily in the field of Soviet Studies." Further, it is clear that Carr's views were not without critics and that he saw the achievement of the Soviet Union as the development of the "supreme architectural plan of the leaders, imposed on the country through the innumerable channels at the disposal of the State." At the end of this book is a bibliography of Carr's works. Although not claiming to be exhaustive, it gives the most complete listing of all the sources consulted.

Abramsky claimed that Carr's monumental *History of Soviet Russia* (eleven volumes published at that time) will be why he will be remembered. Carr, according to Abramsky's account "questioned and cross-examined " all the leaders and chief participants of the Russian Revolution, "and asked them for their motives" for various actions they had taken. Like the illustrious Florentine [Machiavelli], Carr could say that he entered the palaces of the Revolution: "and there make bold to speak to them and ask the motives of their actions, and they, in their humanity, reply to me." The answers Carr received "form the backbone" of the history of Russia from 1917 to 1929.

According to Abramsky's account, Carr was also a "man of action" who wrote *Times* editorials during World War I where he explained the need for better understanding of Russia and its place among the nations of the world.

Summary

The information in *Essays in Honor of E. H. Carr* knits together the various "facts" about Carr contained in other biographies. It seems that Carr's early career with the British Foreign Office and particularly his involvement with Russian affairs during the crucial revolutionary times provided the seeds for Carr's life work. Apparently Carr saw the Russian Revolution as a positive movement from a "backward, reactionary country into one of the mighty 'super-powers' of the world." (Abaramsky, op. cit., p. vii). This is obviously a controversial position, and one about which Carr not only wrote scholarly books, but also one which he sought to bring others to through his *Times* editorials.

In order to confirm these leads more research would have to be done. All book reviews should be consulted, and of course, Carr's works themselves should be read. A Google search revealed that E.H. Carr died on November 5, 1982, at 90 years of age.

3.
Analyzing a Document

Here we have an exercise in weighing historical significance and placing evidence in context. Given an excerpt from a significant historical document, the task is to annotate and summarize it in the following manner:

Introduction

Provide the background information necessary to understand the document. Then draw some conclusions about the meaning and significance of the document you are editing. Explain what it reveals about the period in which it was written and its role in the events of the day.

The Text

Present the text of the document and identify each obscure reference or person mentioned in the text in a footnote. Some documents may have several things to be identified while others may have none. Edgar Allan Poe hardly needs to be identified. Robert Peary, the first man to the North Pole, does.

Conclusion and Bibliography

Attach a bibliography of the works that have been the most useful in understanding the document and its placement in its own time.

ANALYZING A DOCUMENT: PRESIDENT U. S. GRANT'S STATE OF THE UNION MESSAGE ON DECEMBER 5, 1876

Introduction

The parting message of Ulysses S. Grant (1822-1885) as the 18th President of the United States (1869-1877) marks the end of a famous and controversial career. His brilliant military strategies during the Civil War won him the rank of full General in 1866, the first U. S. citizen to achieve that distinction since Washington.

President Andrew Johnson, realizing that Grant's popularity could be an asset if he were an ally, appointed Grant as an interim Secretary of War in 1867 and thus drew him into the political forum of the country. However, the Senate refused to sanction the removal of the existing War Secretary, Edwin Stanton, who was responsible for enforcing the Reconstruction policy, which Johnson opposed. Grant evaded Johnson's bid to test the constitutionality of the Tenure of Office Act by withdrawing from the office. This action defined Grant's alignment with the radical Republicans. Thus, the radical Republicans, capitalizing on Grant's popular strength, chose him as their candidate in 1868 and he was elected to the presidency over the Democratic candidate, Horatio Seymour.

From the beginning of his administration Grant involved himself with people who were to undermine his credibility and confidence. His appointment of Alexander T. Stewart, a wealthy New Yorker, as Secretary of the Treasury was immediately challenged. Senator Carl Schurz confronted Grant with the problem of Stewart's business interests, which conflicted with his role as Treasurer, and Stewart ultimately resigned.

Grant's choice of Elihu B. Washburne as his first Secretary of State was also of short duration (only six days), but the decision to remove Washburne was Grant's. Washburne's replacement, Hamilton Fish, was to serve Grant for the full administration. Fish became Grant's good friend and confidant as well as a distinguished statesman. Most of the other men around Grant were not as virtuous as Fish. Financiers Jay Gould and James

Fisk deceptively sought the support of Grant's administration in an attempt to corner the gold market in 1869. They had direct access to Grant through another financier, Abel Rathbone Corbin, who was married to Grant's sister Virginia. The attempt failed when government gold was released for sale, and the result was Black Friday, when thousands of people were financially ruined. Congress voted to investigate the panic and scrutinized Grant's administration. General Butterfield, the Assistant Secretary of the Treasury, who was playing the market himself, was forced to resign. Despite this incident, Grant was re-elected easily over Horace Greeley in 1872.

Grant's tenure as President generally suffered from bitter partisan politics. The Reconstruction program of the radicals was punitive in nature and the commercial/industrial interests were the main legislative concerns. Accusations of corruption were to follow Grant through the end of his administration, when his Secretary of War, William W. Belknap, and his private secretary, Orville E. Babcock, were implicated in scandals. Secretary Belknap was impeached, although he had already given Grant his resignation, because he had received bribes from investors who were making money on an Indian trading post, at the expense of the Indians. Orville Babcock was involved in a whiskey fraud. Grant, in loyalty to Babcock, wanted to take the witness chair to protect him. Instead, he testified indirectly from the White House and Babcock was acquitted. He would have welcomed Babcock back to his job except for the warning and advice of Hamilton Fish, who persuaded Grant to dismiss Babcock. Fish had evidence that implicated Babcock in the gold speculation that lead to Black Friday. There were also problems with Vice President Colfax and his ties to Credit Mobilier scandal.

After leaving office in 1877, Grant made a much-heralded tour of the world. In 1880 an attempt to secure another Republican nomination for President failed. After losing most of his money in a fraudulent private banking business, Grant wrote his *Personal Memoirs* to help provide for his family. He died in 1885 just after completing his *Memoirs*. The two-volume set, published by Mark Twain, was a great success and ultimately brought in over $481,0000 in royalties.

Text

The following are the first paragraphs of the State of the Union Message of President Ulysses S. Grant to Congress at the end of his second and final term. Dated December 5, 1876.[1]

Executive Mansion, December 5, 1876.[2]

To the Senate and House of Representatives:

In submitting my eighth and last annual message to Congress it seems proper that I should refer to and in some degree recapitulate the events and official acts of the past eight years.

It was my fortune, or misfortune, to be called to the office of Chief Executive without any previous political training. From the age of 17 I had never even witnessed the excitement attending a Presidential campaign but twice antecedent to my own candidacy, and at but one of them was I eligible as a voter.[3]

Under such circumstances it is but reasonable to suppose that errors of judgment must have occurred. Even had they not, differences of opinion between the Executive, bound by an oath to the strict performance of his duties, and writers and debaters must have arisen. It is not necessarily evidence of blunder on the part of the Executive because there are these differences of views. Mistakes have been made, as all can see and I admit, but it seems to be oftener in the selections made of the assistants[4] appointed to aid in carrying out the various duties of administering the Government in nearly every case selected without a personal acquaintance with the appointee, but upon recommendations of the representatives chosen directly by the people.[5] It is impossible, where so many trusts are to be allotted, that the right parties should be chosen in every instance. History shows that no Administration from the time of Washington to the present has been free from these mistakes. But I leave comparisons to history, claiming only that I have acted in every instance from a conscientious desire to do what was right, constitutional, within the law, and for the very best interests of the whole people. Failures have been errors of judgment, not of intent . . .

---

[1]James D. Richardson (ed.), *A Compilation of the Messages and Papers of the Presidents 1789-1897* (10 vols. Washington, DC 1896-99), vol. 7, pp. 399-413.

[2]Written after the November, 1876 election of Rutherford B. Hayes as President.

[3]Grant was in the army for most of his adult life and his only official ballot was cast in Missouri for James Buchanan in 1856.

[4]Assistant Secretary of the Treasury, General Daniel Butterfield, and Secretary of War, William W. Belknap.

[5]Butterfield was appointed because of Abel Corbin's lobbying and Belknap was appointed because of General Sherman's support.

Conclusion

In this formal and normally impersonal governmental document Grant took his countrymen back to his boyhood and tried to explain how and why things went wrong. After entering the army at 17, except for a brief period, his life was devoted to the military. So Grant claimed that he became the Chief Executive "without any previous political training." He ignored the fact that his political interests and involvement had become increasingly intense since 1864.

While placing the blame only indirectly on himself, and more directly and "oftener" on his "assistants," who he asserted were not chosen directly by him, he was removing the cause of any wrongdoing away from himself on two levels. First of all, he did not do anything wrong himself – his "assistants" did. And secondly, he did not choose these "assistants" personally, but rather relied on the suggestions and nominations of others. Apparently, Grant was not referring to Babcock, but only to Butterfield and Belknap, as Babcock was a personal choice and Grant was instrumental in his acquittal.

The rest of the text represents much more than an apology. In fact it discusses and recapitulates the events of Grant's eight years in office. He speaks of being squarely behind the Congressional reconstruction measures, which allowed the victors an equal voice over the defeated Confederacy in controlling the South's government. Grant also spoke about being "proud" of his support of the Fifteenth Amendment, which said that no man should be denied from voting because of race (ratified on March 30, 1870). Grant further discussed the avarice of the white man toward the Indians. He was very clear that treaties were violated in search of precious metals and discussed the case of the Sioux and the Black Hills.

The President took Congress to task for reducing consular service, especially in Bolivia, Equador, and Colombia, and for providing only for chargés d'affaires instead of ministers in Portugal, Denmark, Greece, Switzerland and Paraguay. He asked that this decision be reconsidered, as the "loss of influence and importance" were not worth the saving of funds.[6]

Grant completed his message with a discussion on the individual cabinet departments and a hope for the building of permanent halls to house the exhibits of the Centennial Exposition at Philadelphia in the Capital. He then brought up a great disappointment – the failure of the Senate to allow him to annex Santo Domingo. It was on this island that "the emancipated race of the South might have found a congenial home."[7]

Grant ended his message as follows:

"With the present term of Congress my official life terminates. It is not probable that the public affairs will ever again receive attention from me further than as a citizen of the Republic."[8]

This is interesting in light of his 1880 attempt at the Presidential nomination.

This document, particularly because of the introductory paragraphs, was regarded as an embarrassing episode in the life of a strong man who had become weak. Grant's discussion of his life and his weakness was without equal until President Nixon gave his own version of "I'm sorry, but . . . "ninety-eight years later. However, I agree with William S. McFeely, a Grant biographer, that taken as a whole, Grant's message was a rare moment of insight into the human element of a President of the United States, a man who was trying to understand his circumstance.[9]

The era of the Grant Administration stands as one of the low points of our Republic. Scandals, impeachments, graft, carpetbaggers, the Ku Klux Klan, Mr. Gould and Mr. Tweed, all played a role in making those years a national disgrace. President Grant's final State of the Union message is still very worthy of study as it reveals much about the period in which it was framed.

---

[6]Richardson, *Compilation of Messages and Papers of Presidents*, p. 402.
[7]Ibid., p. 412.
[8]Ibid., p. 413.
[9]William S. McFeeley, *Grant: A Biography* (New York: W. W. Norton & Co., 1981), p. 445.

BIBLIOGRAPHY

Grant, Ulysses S. *The Papers of Ulysses S. Grant.* Edited by John Y. Simon. 8 vols. Carbondale: Illinois University Press, 1967.

_____, *Personal Memoirs of U. S. Grant.* New York: C. C. Webster Co., 1885 – 86.

Grant, Ulysses S., 3rd. *Ulysses S. Grant, Warrior and Statesman.* New York: William Morrow & Co., 1969.

Grodinsky, Julius. *Jay Gould: His Business Career, 1867–1892.* Philadelphia: University of Pennsylvania Press, 1957.

McFeely, *William S. Grant: A Biography.* New York: W. W. Norton & Co., 1981.

Mantell, Martin E. Johnson, *Grant and the Politics of Reconstruction.* New York: Columbia University Press, 1973.

Nevins, Allan, *Hamilton Fish: The Inner History of the Grant Administration.* 2vols. New York: Dodd Mead & Co., 1936.

Richardson, James D. (ed.) A *Compilation of the Messages and Papers of The Presidents 1789-1897.* 10 vols. Washington, DC 1896 – 1899 (7: 399-413).

Young, John Russell. *Around the World with General Grant.* New York: the American News Co., 1879.

4.

Criticizing an Argument

Read the excerpts from the enclosed article by historian, Barbara Tuchman—

"The Decline of Quality"

Summarize her main points and then discuss whether her evidence proves them. Identify any facts that help disprove or that can be used to support a different viewpoint. Use Tuchman's evidence to agree or disagree with her main thesis.

Excerpts from

THE DECLINE OF QUALITY

by Barbara W. Tuchman

The New York Times Sunday Magazine, November 2, 1980

A question raised by our culture of the last two or three decades is whether quality in product and effort has become a vanishing element of current civilization. The work "quality" has, of course, two meanings: first, the nature or essential characteristic of something, as in "His voice has the quality of command;" second, a condition of excellence implying fine quality as distinct from poor quality. The second, obviously, is my subject. . . .

. . . . let me say that quality, as I understand it, means investment of the best skill and effort possible to produce the finest and most admirable result possible. Its presence or absence in some degree characterizes every man-made object, service, skilled or unskilled labor-laying bricks, painting a picture, ironing shirts, practicing medicine, shoemaking, scholarship, writing a book. You do it well or you do it half-well. Materials are sound and durable or they are sleazy; method is painstaking or whatever is easiest. Quality is achieving or reaching for the highest standard as against being satisfied with the sloppy or fraudulent. It is honesty of purpose as against catering to cheap or sensational sentiment. It does not allow compromise with the second-rate.

When Michelangelo started work on the Sistine Chapel ceiling, five friends who were painters came to assist him and advise him in the techniques of fresco, in which they were practiced and he was not. Finding their work not what he desired, he resolved to accomplish the whole task by himself, locked the doors of the chapel until his friends gave up and went home, and through four painful years on a scaffold carried the work to completion, as Vasari tells us, "with the utmost solicitude, labor and study." That is what makes for quality-and its cost-and what helped to make Michelangelo one of the greatest artists, if not, as some think the greatest, of all time. Creating quality is self-nourishing. . . . Genius and effort go together, or if they do not, the genius will be wasted.

Quality, however, can be attained without genius. Art, in any case, is a slippery area for discussion of the problem, because values in the perception of art change radically from one generation to another. Everyone knows how the French Impressionists were scorned when they first exhibited. . . . Now, in our time, we are confronted by new schools of challenging, not to say puzzling, expression. In some individuals among the moderns, quality is emphatic because it is individual: in Louise Nevelson's impressive and innovative work, for example; in the intensity of loneliness in Hopper's mature paintings. With regard to the schools-as distinct from individuals-of Pop Art, Abstract Expressionism, Minimalism, hard-edge, scrawny-edge and whatnot, the two criteria of quality-intensive effort and honesty of purpose-often seem missing. The paintings seem thin if not empty; one feels nothing behind the surface of the canvas. By contrast, behind the glow and mystery of a Turner, for instance, a whole world of ships and storms and eerie seas and men laboring over mountain passes stretches the imagination far beyond the canvas. It occurs to me to wonder whether museums hang the modern abstracts, and the public crowds to see them, in some vast pretense of see-ing something where there is nothing; that in the present state of our cul-ture, many do not know the difference.

Here we must confront the contentious question whether quality is something inherent in a given work or something socially induced . . . . In architecture there is something inherently right in certain proportions of windows to wall space, or for example in the Double Cube Room at Wilton House in England. One may be an architectural illiterate and still recognize, indeed *feel*, the perfection. Any kind of illiterate will recognize a difference in quality between, let us say, Matisse's exhilarating interiors and hotel art of little waifs with big black eyes, or between Michelangelo's marble Moses or David and that school of sculpture which consists of jigsaw puzzles lying on a museum floor, or, alternatively, the ceramic Snow Whites and Bambis. . . .

. . . . The difference is not only a matter of artistic skill, but of intent. Although the Moses and David are period pieces, they are timeless, uni-versal, noble. They were intended to be-and they are-supreme. The oth-ers fall considerably short of that measure because they are designed for lesser reasons: the ceramic princesses and companions for commercial appeal to cheap sentiment . . . .

. . . . These examples represent the posing of extremes in which quali-ty versus nonquality is unmistakable. If I come closer, however, and sug-gest that quality is inherent in, let us say, the stark, exquisite fiction of Jean Rhys but not in "Princess Daisy," in New England's white-steepled churches but not in Howard Johnson's orange-roofed eateries, in the film "Ninotchka" but not in "Star Wars," in Fred Astaire but not in Johnny Carson, I shall be pelted with accusations of failure to understand that what was once considered quality has given way under a change of social values to appreciation of new qualities and new values; that the admirers of the ceramic dolls and trash fiction and plastic furniture and television talk and entertainment shows with their idiotic laughter find something in these objects and diversions that means quality to *them*-in short, that quality is subjective. Yes, indeed, just as there are men who believe and loudly insist they are sober and who stumble and weave and pass out five minutes later. The judgment is subjective but the condition is not.

Contemporary life undeniably marks many improvements over the past, in freedom and nonconformity and most strikingly in material wel-fare. Such fine devices as the microchips that govern computer systems, a lifesaving mechanism like the cardiac pacemaker, drip-water tech-niques that permit arid-zone agriculture and a thousand other develop-ments that have added to human efficiency and well-being may be cited as evidence of modern quality. Nevertheless, these are technological and seem to me to belong to a different scheme of things from the creative components of civilized life.

In two other areas, morals and politics, loss of quality is widely felt, but as I am not sure that the present level in these areas is much lower than at many other periods in history, I shall leave them out of the discussion.

In labor and culture, standards are certainly lower. Everyone is conscious of the prevalence of slipshod performance in clerical, manual and bureaucratic work. Much of it is slow, late, inaccurate, inefficient, either from lack of training or lack of caring or both. . . .

. . . . Even more striking is recognition that no such letter could have been written from a reasonably literate office 10 or 15 years ago. The decline has been precipitate, perhaps as one result of the student movements of the 1960s, when learning skills was renounced in favor of "doing your own thing" or consciousness-raising and other exercises in self-fulfillment. It is good for the self to be fulfilled but better if coping skills are acquired first.

In culture the tides of trash rise a little higher by the week: in fast foods and junky clothes and cute greeting cards, in films devoted nowadays either to sadism or teenagers and consequently either nasty or boring; in the frantic razzle-dazzle of Bloomingdale's and its proliferating imitators; in endless paperbacks of sex and slaughter, Gothics and westerns; in the advertising of sensation-fiction which presents each book as the ultimate in horror, catastrophe, political plot or world crime, each by an unknown author who is never heard from again-fortunately.

Examining the evidence, one could apply a system of Q and non-Q for quality . . . .

. . . . Quality is undeniably, though not necessarily, related to class, not in its nature but in circumstances. In former times, the princely patron had the resources in wealth and power to commission the finest workmanship, materials and design. Since his motive was generally self-glorification, the result was as beautiful and magnificent as he could command: in crystal and gold and tapestry, in exquisite silks and brocades, in the jeweled and enameled masterpieces of Cellini, the carved staircases of Grinling Gibbons. It is also true that cities and states caused works of equal value to be created not for individual glory but for the good of the whole, as in the Greek temples and theaters, the Colosseum of Rome, the Gothic cathedrals, the public parks of London.

The decline that has since set in has a good historical reason: The age of privilege is over and civilization has passed into the age of the masses. The many exceptions that can be made to this statement do not invalidate it. No change takes place wholly or all at once and many components of privilege and of capitalist control remain functioning parts of society and will, I expect, continue as such for some time. Nevertheless, the turn has taken place, with the result that our culture has been taken over by commercialism directed to the mass market and necessarily to mass taste. De Tocqueville stated the problem, already appearing in his time, succinctly when he wrote, "When only the wealthy had watches they were very good ones; few are now made that are worth much but everyone has one in his pocket."

In the absence of the princely patron, the public is now the consumer, or if government is the patron, it is answerable to the public. The criterion for the goods and services and arts that society produces is the pleasure and purchasing power of the greatest number, not of the most discerning. Therein lies the history of non-Q. Arts and luxuries may still be directed to the few and most discerning, but when the dominant culture is mass-directed and the rewards in money and celebrity go with it, we have to consider whether popular appeal will become the governing criterion and gradually submerge all but isolated rocks of quality. . . .

. . . . Quality cannot be put down altogether. As the would-be philosopher said of cheerfulness, it keeps breaking in, and I suspect always will. It appears in the crafts movement that, in a reaction to floods of the tawdry, has been expanding in the last decade, producing fine handwoven fabrics and handmade utensils and ornaments of pottery, glass and wood. There are art and design in these and individual skills that make for Q. We come across Q here and there is every field of endeavor, from a symphony orchestra to a well-run grocery and on the covers of the *Audubon* bimonthly magazine. For all its appearances we are grateful and by them encouraged, yet we have to recognize that the prevailing tendency is non-Q. This is not confined to the taste of the masses It reaches into the richer ranks, where purchasing power has outdistanced cultivated judgment. Persons in this difficulty tend to buy purses and scarfs and various garments-even sheets-adorned with the designer's or manufacturer's initials in the illusion that, without risking individual judgment, they are thus acquiring the stamp of Q. In fact, they are merely proclaiming that they lack reliable taste of their own. . . .

. . . . Most of the products of non-Q have the economic excuse that they supply needs to pocketbooks that can afford them. An entire level of society has arisen that can now afford to obtain goods, services and entertainment formerly beyond its means. Consequently these are now produced at a price level attractive to the greatest number of consumers and likewise at a cultural level, or level of taste, that presumably the greatest number wants or will respond to. Whether the merchandiser or advertiser is invariably a good judge of what the public wants is open to doubt. Whereas one used naively to believe that, under the infallible test of profit, business knew what it was doing, we have now witnessed the most monumental goof in business history committed by the very king of American enterprise, the auto industry. If Detroit with all its resources errs, can the rest be far behind?

A question that puzzles me is why inexpensive things must be ugly; why walking through the aisles in a discount chain store causes acute discomfort in the esthetic nerve cells. I have heard it suggested that raucous colors and hideous decoration are meant to distract the purchaser's eye from shoddy workmanship, but since that only results in a remedy worse than the disease, it cannot be the whole explanation. . . . The automobile companies thought they knew too, and they were so wrong that the taxpayer is now bailing them out in survival loans and unemployment insurance to the workers they had to let go.

I do not see why the presumption cannot be made the other way: that the consumer would respond to good design rather than bad, and to quality insofar as it can be mass-produced, rather than junk. The answer will doubtless be that when this experiment has been tried the mass of consumers fails to respond. For this failure, I believe, two institutions of our culture are largely to blame: education and advertising.

We have some superb schools, public and private, in the country but the dominant tendency, once again, is non-Q. Education for the majority has slipped to a level undemanding of effort, satisfied with the least, lacking respect for its own values, and actually teaching very little. We read in the press that, despite the anxious concern and experiments of educators, college-entrance scores are sinking and the national rate of schoolchildren reading at below-grade levels hovers at 50 percent. The common tendency is to blame television, and while I suppose that the two-minute attention span it fosters, and the passive involvement of the viewer, must negatively affect the learning process, I suspect something more basic is at fault.

That something, I believe, lies in new attitudes toward both teaching and learning. Schoolchildren are not taught to work. Homework is frivolous or absent. The idea has grown that learning must be fun; students must study what they like, therefore courses have largely become elective. Work is left to the highly motivated, and failure for the others does not matter because, owing to certain socially concerned but ill-conceived rules, students in many school systems cannot be flunked. Except by the few who learn because they cannot be stopped, the coping skills society needs are not acquired by the promoted failures, and the gulf between the few and the mass will widen.

Further, one becomes aware through occasional glimpses into curriculums, that subject matter makes increasing concessions to junk. Where are the summer reading lists and book reports of former years? A high-school student of my acquaintance in affluent suburbia was recently assigned by his English teachers, no less, to watch television for a week and keep a record on 3-by-5 index cards of what he had seen. This in the literature of Shakespeare to Mark Twain, Jane Austen to J.D. Salinger! How will the young become acquainted with quality if they are not exposed it? . . . .

. . . . Advertising augments the condition. From infancy to adulthood, advertising is the air Americans breathe, the information we absorb, almost without knowing it. It floods our minds with pictures of perfection and goals of happiness easy to attain. . . . Moreover, all the people engaged in these delights are beautiful. Dare I suggest that this is not the true world?

We are feeding on foolery, of which a steady diet, for those who feed on little else, cannot help but leave a certain fuzziness of perceptions.

When it comes to standards of labor, the uncomfortable fact must be faced that decline in quality of work is connected with the rise in the security of the worker. No one likes to admit this because it is depressing and because it does not fit into the sentimental conviction that all's well that is meant well, that good things have only good results. The unhappy fact is that they have mixed results. Work may be a satisfaction to those who can choose their own line of endeavor and who enjoy what they do, but for the majority work is a more or less disagreeable necessity. Therefore, when holding a job no longer depends upon quality of performance but on union rules and bureaucratic protections, the incentive to excellent work is reduced. Like the failing student who cannot be flunked, the inadequate worker cannot be fired, short of some extreme dereliction. If he is laid off or quits for reasons of his own, unemployment insurance provides a temporary substitute for the pay envelope and, in the long run, the various supports of social welfare preclude destitution.

No one this side of the lunatic fringe suggests that these rights and protections of labor should be abandoned or weakened because loss of quality has been part of their price. Gain in one aspect of society generally means loss in another, and social gain in the well-being of the masses has been the major development of the last two centuries. We have put a floor under misery in the West and few would wish it removed because its measures have been abused. The privileged abuse their opportunities too, by monopolies, trusts, graft, bribery, tax evasion, pollution-and with far higher returns. At whatever cost, the working class has obtained access to comforts and pleasures, possessions and vacations that have changed immeasurably not only their lives but the whole of our economy and culture. On balance, this is social progress, but let us not suppose it has been unalloyed.

Other factors have played a part: The alienating nature of the assembly line and mass production is one, but this has been present since the Industrial Revolution. The great change has come with the complacency on the whole, in America-a comfortable society (previous to present inflation and recession). As in education, the change has been in attitude. The pressures and needs that once drove us have relaxed. Today's watchword is "Why knock yourself out?" The Asians in our midst-Koreans who put a whole family to work in a grocery of neat, washed, fresh produce, and stay open for 24 hours-exemplify the difference. . . .

. . . . In fact, elitism is the equivalent of quality. Without it, management of everything would be on a par with the United States Postal Service, which, mercifully, is not yet quite the case. Difference in capacity does exist and superiority makes itself felt. It wins the ski race and promotion on the job and admission to the college of its choice. There are A students and D students, and their lives and fortunes will be different. I do not know if egalitarianism applies to horses, but if so how does it account for Seattle Slew and Affirmed sweeping the triple crown;

and if all are equal, why do we hold horse races? Given the evidence of daily life, the egalitarian credo must be difficult to maintain and succeeds, I imagine, in deceiving chiefly its advocates.

However, because egalitarianism obviously appeals to those least likely to excel-and they are many-its appeal is wide, and not altogether harmless. It sponsors mediocrity, which, as we learned a few years ago on the occasion of President Nixon's nomination of Judge G. Harold Carswell to the Supreme Court, has an important constituency in this county. The general criticism of Carswell as mediocre prompted from Senator Roman L. Hruska of Nebraska one of the historic remarks of the century. He did not think Carswell should be disqualified on the grounds of an undistinguished judicial career, because, he said, "Even if he were mediocre, there are a lot of mediocre judges and people and lawyers and they are entailed to a little representation, aren't they?"

The more I ponder this idea of a seat for mediocrity on the Supreme Court, the more it haunts me. The Hruska Principle is only a logical extension, after all, of majority rule, and if carried to its logical conclusion must mean that the mediocre shall inherit the earth. (Carswell was rejected, of course, but for alleged racism, not for mediocrity.)

. . . . I cannot believe we shall founder under the rising tide of incompetence and trash. Perhaps that is merely a matter of temperament; it is difficult to believe in fatality. Although I know we have already grown accustomed to less beauty, less elegance, less excellence-and less hypocrisy, too-yet perversely I have confidence in the opposite of egalitarianism: in the competence and excellence of the best among us. I meet this often enough, if not quite as often as the reverse, to believe that the urge for the best is an element of humankind as inherent as the heartbeat. It does not command society, and it may be crushed temporarily in a period of heavy non-Q, but it cannot be eliminated. If incompetence does not kill us first, Q will continue the combat against numbers. It will not win, but it will provide a refuge for the trash-beleaguered. It will supply scattered beauty, pride in accomplishment, the charm of fine things-and it will win horse races. As long as people exist, some will always strive for the best; some will attain it.

CRITICIZING AN
ARGUMENT

In "The Decline of Quality" Barbara Tuchman addressed a problem "raised by our culture of the last two or three decades."[1] She defined quality as a "condition of excellence" that "means investment of the best skill and effort possible to produce the finest and most admirable result possible." Further, Tuchman claimed that quality, "inherent in a given work," is objective.

Although one might expect a documented work from a historian, Barbara Tuchman made it clear that this article was a presentation of her personal reflections and opinions. Thus, the method was to offer her perspective, one of a perceptive scholar, in the hopes that further factual studies would be stimulated. Thus, this critique is of an informed opinion, which as Tuchman hoped reduces the "hail of censure." The approach in Tuchman's article was to discuss areas where quality has declined, to offer her insights into the how and why of this phenomenon and finally to suggest an answer to the problem.

Art, culture, and labor were cited as the three areas of lowered standards. Of the condition of morals and politics, Tuchman was not certain if our society has reached an historical low point. Interestingly, she felt technology had no place in the discussion. Nevertheless, by her own definition quality is present or absent in "every man-made object, service…" Therefore it certainly is present in the achievements of technology. Indeed the technological advances of the last forty years, from personal computers, the internet, to micro and laser surgery, to men on the moon, represent the "best skill and effort possible" and surely have produced "most admirable results." Unfortunately Barbara Tuchman ignores this important area of human endeavor and consequently shortchanges the extent of quality on the contemporary scene.

The argument for the decline of quality in art is problematic. Tuchman made the point that "values in perception in art change radically from one generation to another." But further she claimed that "quality is something inherent in a given work." Therefore, quality is recognized perfection, and in fact she claimed: "any kind of illiterate will recognize the difference in quality…" If this is the case, why do the "mass of consumers" fail to respond to quality? How can education and advertising be blamed for such a failure if the individual knows the difference? Here Dr. Tuchman seems to have contradicted herself. Her error was in the assumption that any illiterate can distinguish the quality of a *David* by Michelangelo from a ceramic Snow White. Literacy may not be necessary to make such a distinction, but a certain sensitivity is required, and that is not a universal ability. Indeed, Tuchman does not seem to be arguing that sensitivity to quality is a universal ability and that the problem is in the gray areas, i. e., between the dancer and actor Fred Astaire and T. V. talk show personality Johnny Carson, but rather that people who like Carson and "ceramic dolls . . . find something in these objects and diversions that means quality to them-in short, that quality is subjective." But, according to Tuchman, quality is "objective" and recognized by "any kind of illiterate."

In her article Tuchman viewed our culture as overcome with the "tides of trash." The categories of Q and non-Q were proposed, aligning quality with class. Herein Ms. Tuchman saw the historical roots of the decline. Quality was more prevalent in classed societies, whereas in the "age of the masses" it is less apparent. Unfortunately, Ms. Tuchman did not give us any facts to substantiate this claim, so it is difficult to assess. However, the cry is an ancient one. Surely, Pericles would have agreed with her. Nevertheless, he also perceived that building the Acropolis engaged the classes in a unifying and symbolic world. A similar involvement was essential to the creation of the medieval cathedrals as well. While stressing the relationship of quality and class, Tuchman missed a perhaps more significant relationship, that of quality and purpose. Michelangelo did not create the Sistine ceiling because he had to produce that quality of work for the Pope. He had a higher purpose!

Our culture is not altogether devoid of quality according to Tuchman. She cited several examples in the positive vein, from the crafts movement to *Audubon* magazine. But she did not attempt to account for these conditions. These phenomena do not seem to be class related at all. For example, the crafts movement can be viewed as a desire to return to the 'simpler things' of a previous era. In fact most crafts were originally homemade functional items in working class households. I suggest that this perspective on quality is related to a sense of purpose as well. Likewise the designer jeans fad is not tasteless so much because someone's name is stuck on the back, but because blue jeans are supposed to be worn when doing hard work, not when going to an elegant party with a mink coat over them!

Tuchman claimed that non-Q rose as a response to the demands of "an entire level of society" that can now afford "goods, services and entertainment formerly beyond its means." The auto industry was cited as an example of what happens when the producer is the judge of what this buying public wants. The point Tuchman missed here is that the reason people stopped buying American cars is because they were inefficient, costly and shoddily made. This opened the market to foreign imports of better efficiency and quality. Even Henry Ford would have been impressed with the results! (It is interesting to note that some foreign cars are experiencing similar complaints of workmanship since they opened American plants to produce their cars.)

Placing the responsibility for non-Q on education and advertising seems to belie the complexity of the problem, and it does not contribute to Barbara Tuchman's view that elitism is to be equated with quality. I would certainly agree that educational standards have eroded and that advertising presents us with false visions of the good life. However, it seems that the heart of the problem is a kind of inertia, a lack of purpose that manifests itself in a negative work ethic, in the loss of joy in doing things. Education and advertising suffer from this problem as much as the rest of society. Although she does not develop her insights along these lines, Tuchman touched on the point several times, for instance where she says that television fosters "passive involvement" and "schoolchildren are not taught to work." It is the message conveyed by advertising that leads us to believe that "perfection and goals of happiness are easy to attain." It is this lack of purpose that "leads to work being viewed as a more or less disagreeable necessity."

In the end Tuchman attributed the lack of quality to egalitarianism, the evenness of everyone and everything. The solution, which she felt will manifest itself naturally is elitism. However, with elitism, as Tuchman must admit, only a small minority will be concerned with quality. Indeed education and advertising will apparently have little effect on this elite. How can the non-Q of the masses be solved by the emergence of an elite with high standards of Q? The "best" can rise, but the masses will remain, impervious to the supply of "scattered beauty, pride in accomplishment, and the charm of fine things." Unless somehow the elite, be it composed of aristocrats, kings, clergy or poets, conveys to the masses a sense of purpose, quality will remain elusive.

[1]All quotes from Barbara Tuchman, "The Decline of Quality," *The New York Times Sunday Magazine*, November 2, 1980, p. 38–xx.

Watson and the Shark

Painting by John Singleton Copley (1736-1815).
Courtesy of the National Gallery of Art, Washington, D.C.

5.

Art and Literature as Historical Records

In this assignment we closely examine American artist, John Singleton Copley's painting, *Watson and the Shark*. Then write an essay indicating how the work reflects the era in which it was painted, its values, ethics, social conditions, hopes, etc. Refer to the painting as evidence.

As in analyzing and evaluating any piece of historical evidence, you should be interested in the recorder, in this case the artist, as well as the record, the painting. To what extent is the painting an expression of the artist's point of view, experiences, overall outlook?

Finally, briefly compare the artist's treatment of his subject with those of his artist contemporaries and of those artists who immediately followed. Determine whether or not art reflects changes in attitude or practices.

ART AND LITERATURE AS
HISTORICAL RECORDS

Jules David Prown, Copley's biographer and the cataloger of his works, had this to say of the artist's life:

> The unexpected blossoming of a major eighteenth century artist in colonial Boston, a small provincial city precariously perched on the Atlantic seaboard of the vast North American continent, is one of the most remarkable episodes in the history of art.[1]

Born on July 3, 1738, John Singleton Copley was one of three children of an Irish tobacconist who apparently died shortly after his son's birth. Copley's mother remarried ten years later. Her new husband was Peter Pelham, "an engraver, portrait painter, and schoolmaster at Trinity Church."[2] Thus young John was brought into a new environment and into direct contact with an experienced artist and his studio.[3] Clearly Copley's innate artistic talent flourished in such a rich setting, and his world expanded to include other local skillful artists including John Smibert (1688-1751), Robert Feke (c.1705-c. 1750), John Greenwood (1727-1792), and John Badger (1708-1765).[4] These artists were among the best in the colonies and represented a distinct period in American art.[5]

Portraiture during the early colonial days was commissioned for "family enjoyment or political distinction."[6] It was a direct result of the increased prosperity in the colonies that portraits of members of the more substantial families multiplied. Louis Wright claimed that "The number of craftsman who turned out these pictures must have been greater than we are likely to imagine…"[7] These works, with a few notable exceptions including those by the artists mentioned above, were not then catalogued as objects of art or considered as "products of creative minds" but were regarded as "momentos of the dead or gestures of respect and affection for the living." Thus the portraits of the early colonial period were viewed as craft products. However, this did not mean that the artists did not attempt to depict their clients elegantly. Indeed it was "only when the beautiful was appropriated by those in questionable social circumstance was there discussion and debate before the Revolution."[8]

When Copley began painting in 1753, these early colonial artists from whom he had learned so much had all died or dispersed. Working in his now departed stepfather's studio, Copley continued to develop what he had learned, and he began to create a style of his own. His portraits had a "strong and vigorous ruggedness."[9] But beyond stylistic innovations, Copley represented a break with the tradition of portraiture as craft. As early as 1760, he voiced his famous complaint that Americans scorned painting and regarded the art as "no more than any other useful trade."[10]

Copley's fortune took a good turn when in 1769 he married Susanna Farnham Clarke, a wealthy widow, whose father was the British agent for the British East India Company. Consequently, the Clarke family was "distinctly loyalist in its politics." Copley's professional, social, and economic standing rose considerably because of his marriage. He immediately began to acquire property on Beacon Hill. John Hancock lived in a house on land adjacent to Copley's property.[11] Copley continued painting portraits largely commissioned by upper crust Boston families, including one of Thomas Mifflin in 1773. Mifflin was, two years later, to become the Quartermaster General of the Revolutionary Army and subsequently a member of the First Continental Congress."[12] Copley also painted the portraits of Paul Revere and Samuel Adams.

In that same year, 1773, Copley's fortunes took another turn. He was caught in the middle of the politics of Boston, particularly in what resulted in the famous "Tea Party." Richard Clarke, his father-in-law, was a "major consignee of the tea as principal agent for the East India Company."[13] Copley became the mediator between Clarke and the Sons of Liberty, as he knew many of the rebel leaders. He explained Clarke's position as a businessman, and assured the leaders that Clarke was not "in contact with or acting under the orders of the governor."[14] Copley's efforts were obviously not very successful.

In April, 1774, a mob came to Copley's house demanding to see Colonel George Watson of Plymouth, a prominent loyalist, who they had heard was visiting there. Watson had already left the house, but Copley was threatened. In June, 1774, Copley left for England, the rationale for his departure being "his old desire to study in Europe."[15] After the war he was able to claim this as a refuge against charges of Toryism, and thus he was allowed to keep his Boston property even though his family had settled in London by that time.

In England, Copley met Benjamin West, considered by some his equal in art, but later also his rival. Together, the work of Copley and West represents an anticipation of the "flowering of Romantic painting."[16] The first major picture painted after he arrived in London reflected this Romantic mood, it was *Watson and the Shark* (1778, 72½" x 90¼", National Gallery of Art). He actually did three versions: two initial versions in 1778, and a third smaller version in 1782.

This now famous painting was not accepted readily because it did not deal with national or classical heroes. Rather, it depicts an actual event that had occurred thirty years earlier in Havana Harbor. The title character, Brook Watson, actually was attacked by a shark. Watson was later accused of being a loyalist informer. However, the incident portrayed in this painting happened years before the time of the Revolution. Thus, Copley was not making a political statement, but dealt with more basic elements. Copley recreated the event in all its horror. The sharp-jawed shark, the symbol of the dangers of the deep, attacks Watson, while Watson's companions, who are not identified, attempt to rescue him. The scene was Copley's means of introducing the theme of man's battle against the forces of nature. This theme was to become a dominant one in later American art. (Watson lost a leg in the episode and later became Lord Mayor of London. He apparently commissioned the initial versions of the picture. An unusual portrait indeed!)[17]

This picture was the precursor of later Romantic paintings, but it was Copley's first history picture as well. It conveys a realistic approach to history that is not unlike West's. Nevertheless, Copley definitely worked in a different style, emulating Rubens. In addition, Copley's *Watson and the Shark* is unusual in that it represents a historical rendering, not of a significant or heroic event, but the extraordinary maiming of a quite ordinary individual. At the time he painted *Watson and the Shark*, the theme was a more likely subject for sensational pictorial journalism. Certainly Copley was not motivated by such ends. What he most likely was conveying was a normal eighteenth century interest in the distant and the exotic.[18] In light of Watson's later accomplishments, the painting can now also convey a heroic tone with courage and loyalty as its theme.

Copley was never to return to America. He continued painting in England and died there in 1815. Art historians often debate the relative merit of his English and American works, but this debate seems to be more "based on nationalistic rather than artistic considerations."[19] In a more neutral light, Copley represents a bridge between the earlier colonial portrait "craftsmen" and the later Romantic "artists" as the times and circumstances of his own lifetime represent the bridge between the British colonial period and the American frontier period. The colonial portraits were "wooden" compared with Copley's vigorous brush strokes. With Copley's masterful hand the faces and lives of his subjects came alive revealing their distinctive personalities. His portrait of *Paul Revere* (1765-70, 35" x 28½", Boston Museum of Fine Arts) is an excellent example. Revere is pictured sitting at a table with his engraver's tools, apparently contemplating a teapot to be engraved. He is depicted in his working clothes and rather romantically if one considers the lovely folds of his muslin shirt and the meditative look on his face. McLanathan claimed that:

> The painting stands as a landmark in American art not only
> because it expresses the self-confident individualism of those
> who were the major participants in the cause of independence,
> but also because it shows Copley at the height of his powers.[20]

Copley and West, as well as Peale and Stuart, were "artists" with ideals of high art. Copley specifically felt that the artist must remain above political struggles. Thus he left for Europe before the Revolution.[21] It does seem unfortunate that Copley missed the new epoch in America that the Revolution fostered as it brought "an air of importance on a thousand actions" and placed "the seal of destiny in individuals."[22] So it was with Stuart and Peale, but not with Copley, that American public portraiture as history was created. As the leading artists of this new era and genre, Charles Willson Peale (1741-1827) and Gilbert Stuart (1755-1828), they were also swept into the Classical revival movement ushered in by Jefferson. Ultimately the Classical themes were absorbed by a full-fledged Romantic movement in painting.

Inspired by Copley, Samuel F. B. Morse (1791-1872) attempted to revive the splendor of the century. His famous portrait of *Lafayette* (1825-26, 96" x 64", City Hall, New York City) represented the living symbol of the Revolution. An aged Lafayette was depicted by Morse against a sunset sky with the busts of Washington and Franklin by his side.[23] The Romantic Movement reached its zenith in Morse's fellow founding member of the National Academy of Design, Thomas Cole (1801-1848). Cole initiated the landscape painting genre and his work represents the American frontier spirit that was enkindled by the vastness of the land 'fresh from creation' and the 'pioneers struggle for survival' that succeeded in the ordered life of farm and village.[24] Romanticism represented the flowering of that spirit of individualism, so evident in Copley's works and in Copley himself. A spirit that saw its expression in portraits by an artist rather than by an unknown craftsman, and in the vivid rendering of a strange, frightening and obscure moment in history in *Watson and the Shark.*

Copley also stands in the center of the encounter between art and nationality. His departure from America was considered a betrayal by many who came to view his work in England as a deterioration from its high point in America. However, for Copley, who valued the art above all, it was a necessary and positive move. In 1775 he wrote: "I shall stand amongst the first of the artists that shall have lead that country (America) to the knowledge and cultivation of the fine arts."[25]

FOOTNOTES

[1]Jules David Prown, *John Singleton Copley*, Vol. 1, In America 1738-1774
(Cambridge: Harvard University Press, 1966), p. 1

[2] Ibid., p. 8.

[3]Ibid., p. 9.

[4]Ibid., pp. 10 – 14.

[5] Ibid., p. 15.

[6]Neil Harris, *The Artist in American Society: The Formative Years 1790-1862*
(New York: George Braziller, 1966), p. 6.

[7]Louis B. Wright, *The Cultural Life of the American Colonies 1607-1763*
(New York: Harper & Row Torchbook, 1962), p. 208.

[8] Ibid., p. 7.

[9] Prown, *Copley*, Vol. 1, p. 28.

[10]Harris, *The Artist in American Society*, p. 8.

[11]Prown, *Copley*, Vol. 1, pp. 61-63.

[12]Ibid., p. 63.

[13] Ibid., p. 91.

[14]Ibid.

[15]Ibid., p. 93.

[16]Richard McLanathan, *The American Tradition in the Arts*
(New York: Harcourt, Brace & World, 1968), p. 99.

[17]Prown, *Copley*, Vol. 2, p. 274.

[18]Ibid., pp. 272-274.

[19]Ibid., pp. 383-384.

[20]McLanathan, *The American Tradition in the Arts*, p. 92.

[21]Harris, *The Artist in American Society*, p. 15.

[22]Ibid., pp. 16-17.

[23]McLanathan, *The American Tradition in the Arts*, p. 23.

[24]Ibid.

[25]Harris, *The Artist in American Society*, p. 25.

BIBLIOGRAPHY

Harris, Neil. *The Artist in American Society:*
The Formative Years 1790-1862. New York: George Braziller, 1966.

McLanathan, Richard. *The American Tradition in the Arts.*
New York: Harcourt, Brace & World, 1968.

Prown, Jules David, *John Singleton Copley*,
Vol. 1, In America 1738-1774; Vol. 2, In England 1774-1815.
Cambridge: Harvard University Press, 1966.

Wright, Louis B. *The Cultural Life of the American Colonies 1607-1763*.
New York: Harper & Row Torchbook, 1962.

6.

Utilizing Statistics as Historical Data

Here we are presented with a statistical problem. We are asked to find the infant mortality rates for the United Kingdom from 1961-1978.

In addition to establishing a statistical chart, briefly respond to the following:

1. What does the statistic mean? Briefly describe what was counted and who did the counting. (Most volumes of statistics describe the sources before giving the statistical tables).

2. What are the significant variations over time? Does the figure for any one year appear especially significant? If so, explain it.

3. List problems you encountered in finding the statistics or in making them usable.

TABLE 1

INFANT MORTALITY RATES*
UNITED KINGDOM**
1961-1978

YEAR	RATE
1961	20.885
1962	21.819
1963	21.568
1964	20.857
1965	19.590
1966	19.235
1967	18.168
1968	17.653
1969	17.078
1970	16.649
1971	16.128
1972	14.591
1973	13.429
1974	12.352
1975	11.190
1976	9.776
1977	9.283
1978	9.133

* Rate of infant deaths per 1,000 live births in same year.

** England/Wales, Northern Ireland, and Scotland.

Source: *Demographic Yearbook of the United Nations*
(United Nations, Statistical Office, Department of Economic
and Social Affairs, 1965, 1970, 1973, 1980 editions.)

UTILIZING STATISTICS AS
HISTORICAL RECORD

Table 1 presents the infant mortality rates for the years 1961 through 1978 in the United Kingdom, including England/Wales, Scotland, and Northern Ireland. The figures were taken from the *Demographic Yearbook of the United Nations*. Four editions were used to accumulate these figures: the 1961-1965 figures are from the 1965 edition,[1] the 1966-1969 figures are from the 1970 edition,[2] the 1970 figure is from the 1973 edition,[3] and the 1971-1978 figures are from the 1980 edition.[4]

The information was originally obtained from civil registers.[5] It was collected by the United Nations Statistical Office, which received the data on monthly and annual questionnaire forms submitted by governmental agencies.[6] The methods of collection and computation of the data were uniform throughout all the editions used.

The United Nations Statistical Office rated the United Kingdom data as reliable, in that it is virtually complete since at least 90% of the infant deaths were represented.[7] For England and Wales the data was tabulated by date of occurrence; it was tabulated by date of registration for Northern Ireland and Scotland.[8] The method of tabulation by date of registration affects the reliability of the data. On one hand there could be a bias on the side of mortality rates if the infant death registration was more complete than the live birth registrations. If the reverse situation was the case, i.e., there was a time lag in reporting infant deaths, but the live births were reliably registered, there would be a bias in the opposite direction. The United Nations Statistical Office claimed that: "If both infant deaths and live births are tabulated by date of registration, it should be noted that deaths tend to be more promptly reported than births."[9]

These infant mortality rates were computed as the number of reported deaths of infants under one year of age per 1,000 live births in the same year.[10] The statistics indicate an overall downward trend in the infant mortality rate from a rate of 20.885 deaths per 1,000 live births in 1961 to a rate of 9.133 deaths per 1,000 live births in 1978. The first two years cited, 1961 and 1962, show the only increase in the infant mortality rate, and this appears to be significant, as the rate did not return to below the 1961 level until 1964. Thereafter, the variation of decrease in the rate is between .355

and 1.537, excluding the last years of 1977 and 1978. In this case the differential was .150 and may represent a bottoming out of the rate. Further research would be necessary to substantiate such a claim, and to determine the reason for the earlier increase in the rate noted above.

FOOTNOTES

[1]United Nations, Statistical Office, Department of Economic and Social Affairs, *Demographic Yearbook 1965*, 17th Issue (New York: United Nations Publishing Service, 1966), p. 728.

[2]United Nations, Statistical Office, Department of Economic and Social Affairs, *Demographic Yearbook 1970*, 22nd Issue (New York: United Nations Publishing Service, 1971), p. 650.

[3]United Nations, Statistical Office, Department of Economic and Social Affairs, *Demographic Yearbook 1973*, 25th Issue (New York: United Nations Publishing Service, 1974), p. 259.

[4]United Nations, Statistical Office, Department of Economic and Social Affairs, *Demographic Yearbook 1980*, 32nd Issue (New York: United Nations Publishing Service, 1982), p. 348.

[5]Ibid., p. 40.

[6]Ibid., p. 3.

[7]Ibid., p. 40.

[8]Ibid., p. 359.

[9]Ibid., p. 41.

[10]Ibid., p. 40.

BIBLIOGRAPHY

In a research library, many kinds of statistics are kept in the same area of the reference section. Among them are:

U.N.: *Statistical Abstract of the United States.*
Historical Statistics of the United States.
Long-Term Economic Growth 1860-1970.
Employment and Earnings 1909-1978.
Vital Statistics of the U. S.
U. K. International: Mitchell, *Abstract of British Historical Statistics.*
Mitchell, *European Historical Statistics 1750-1950.*
U.N.: *Compendium of Social Statistics.*
U.N.: *Statistical Yearbook.*
U.N.: *Yearbook of National Accounts Statistics.*
The Statesman's Yearbook.
U.N.: *Demographic Yearbook.*

7.

Research Paper: The Harlem River Ship Canal

This exercise is to research and write a lengthy
essay on a historical subject. Present a different
interpretation of the material, rather than
a list of items copied from various sources.
Originality in your thesis is essential
but all interpretations must be supported
with solid evidence.

The question:

**What is The Harlem River Ship Canal
and how did it come to be?**

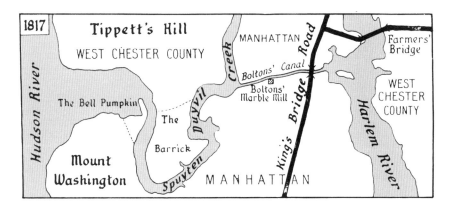

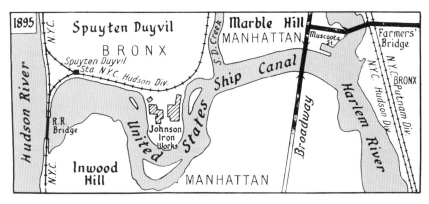

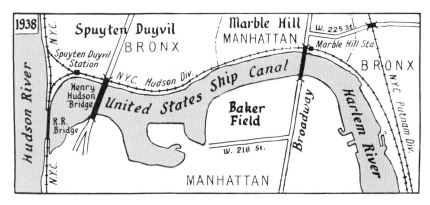

The United States Ship Canal (Harlem River Ship Canal)
through the years.
John Forsyth, Cartographer.
The Bronx County Historical Society Collection.

THE HARLEM RIVER SHIP CANAL

by Gary Hermalyn

In 1893 an article in *The New York Times* noted:

> The Harlem Ship Canal is an enterprise of which the oldest inhabitant of New York cannot remember the origin and of which the youngest inhabitant is not likely to see its fulfillment.[1]

This project, which was one hundred and twelve years in the making, is testimony to the tenacity of an idea. No one person or association led the crusade. Despite the ravages of nature, war, political and legal problems, economic disasters and private opposition, the initial plan to build a canal connecting the Hudson and Harlem Rivers was finally carried out.

The reasons behind the canal are evident upon the examination of a mid-nineteenth century map of the City of New York. While Manhattan was an island, the stream on its northern boundary was not fully navigable. To promote more efficient commercial shipping to the Harlem River, East River and Long Island Sound, with the resultant wharves and docks and new industry, a canal seemed a natural course. After the Erie Canal was completed, Governor DeWitt Clinton formulated legislation on the canal as the proper outlet for commerce to Long Island Sound.[2] Simply stated, a canal linking the Hudson and Harlem Rivers was a good idea.

Ironically, in spite of the scope of this project, few authors of New York history have paid it much attention. Stephen Jenkins, whose *Story of The Bronx 1639-1912* is the best history on the borough to date, mentioned the ship canal in passing reference to bridges and the surrounding area. *The Great North Side or Borough of The Bronx*, published in 1897, indicated the commercial benefit of the canal, but did not discuss its development.[3] In *The Story of New York*, published in 1964, Susan Lyman mentioned the canal only in regard to Marble Hill, and she noted that it was completed in 1895 ". . . making the waters north of Manhattan navigable and creating a short cut from the Hudson to the East River."[4] J. Thomas Scharf's *History of Westchester County* in 1886 gave the canal project scant notice.[5]

Even historical perspectives devoted to the canal rarely mention its background before the 1870's. Noble E. Whitford's *History of the Barge Canal of New York State* placed the canal's origins in the 1874 Act of Congress.[6] An 1895 *Scientific American* article devoted to the project began the history in 1873 with the River and Harbor Act.[7] An historical overview of the long history of the canal project is rare. One can be found in the 1893 *Report* of the Harlem River and Spuyten Duyvil Association which contained a detailed, although incomplete, chronology of the project to 1886.[8] Only in attorney Fordham Morris's address delivered at the celebration in honor of the opening of the canal in 1895 was the history of the project covered back to 1827.[9]

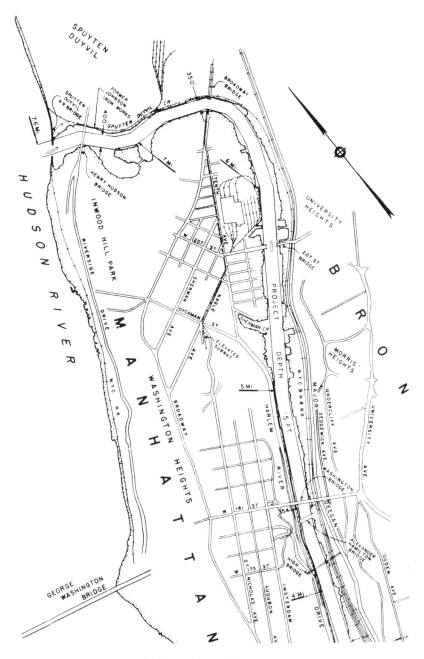

Map of The Harlem River, June 30, 1975.
*Courtesy of the Department of The Army, New York District
Corps of Engineers, New York, New York.*

This study then is devoted to uncovering the facts that surrounded the creation of the Harlem River Ship Canal. It specifically addressed itself to two questions: what factors forced this project to take so long? Was it worth the effort?

The official name for the waterway extending from Spuyten Duyvil to the Harlem River at West 225th Street is designated by the U.S. Army Corps of Engineers as the United States Ship Canal. In the metropolitan region, however, it is known as the Harlem River Ship Canal.[10] Today it is commonly called the Harlem River and few people who traverse its waters either by boat or by foot or vehicle over its bridges realize that it is a man-made canal that they are crossing. Originally there was a waterway through the area called Spuyten Duyvil Creek, and the area on the Bronx side of the canal is still referred to by this name. Reginald Pelham Bolton described the original creek in this way:

> Around this hill the Spuyten Duyvil Creek made its sinuous way, connecting with the two streams that emptied into it on either side of Kingsbridge. That on the east was but a small brook, while the Mosholu on the west received the main supply of water coming from the Van Cortlandt lake and millpond. The two streams thus made of Kingsbridge or the Indian "Papirinemin" an island, and a most desirable spot for Indian occupation, protected by the waters, sheltered by the hills, fertile of soil, with abundant opportunity for fishing and oystering.[11]

There are several versions of how Spuyten Duyvil Creek got its name. The most likely source for the name, according to historian John McNamara, is ". . . a 1647 reference to a gushing fountain of fresh water that poured in to the creek." The Dutch settlers called it "Devil's Spout" or "Spuit den Duyvil." The original creek virtually disappeared under the fill from the canal construction.[12]

The Spuyten Duyvil Creek, a tidal waterway that emptied into the Hudson River, ran along the northern tip of Manhattan. At Kingsbridge it met the Harlem River, another tidal waterway which separated Manhattan along its northeast border from the mainland.[13] In 1813 Robert Macomb built a dam across the Harlem River. As the dam was without a draw, it cut off navigation of the river and caused the area of Kingsbridge to become a tidal mill pond.[14] Upset over these problems the farmers north of the dam took the matter into their own hands and on September 14, 1838, tore down the dam and reopened the river for navigation. Macomb took them to court. The courts, however, upheld the farmers and maintained that:

> Harlem River is an arm of the sea and a public highway, that Macomb's Dam was a nuisance and the Westchester farmers were justified in its abatement.[15]

In 1848, as part of the Croton aqueduct system for New York City, the

High Bridge was completed, one hundred feet above the Harlem River, and about midway in its course. The High Bridge was built to allow navigation to the upper river,[16] and kept the gravity feed of the aqueduct intact.

As early as 1826 a company had been incorporated to construct a canal connecting the Hudson River and the Harlem River through Spuyten Duyvil. On April 18, 1826, the Harlaem River Canal Company was incorporated by the New York State Legislature. At that time the company was given the authority to cut a canal. It was not, however, an exclusive privilege and the canal had to be built within two years.[17] In April 1827 the name seems to have been changed to the Harlaem River Canal Company, and the term was extended for four years from that date.[18] The City of New York Common Council voted to grant the Harlaem River Canal Company the right to construct the canal on July 16, 1827. The Common council also demanded a $30,000 deposit at the time as "security for the due performance of their agreement."[19]

According to official city records, the Harlaem River Canal Company never got the project underway, although Fordham Morris reported in 1895 that they did expend some efforts.[20] Though the company's time limit was extended several times by the State, the economic crises of the 1830's apparently forced the Harlaem River Canal Company to abandon the project "with great loss to the incorporators and stockholders."[21]

For the next fifteen years the project was dormant. In 1855 the Governor of the State of New York appointed a Harbor Commission which two years later issued a map and a report which included the Harlem River and Spuyten Duyvil Creek. Colonel J. McLeon Murphy, a civil engineer, was asked to make another survey by the City in 1860.[22] Murphy's plan was substantially the same as the one ultimately adopted.[23] In late 1860 the Mayor approved a Common Council resolution authorizing payment for the "dredging of the channel of the Harlem River above High Bridge."[24] This was not work on the canal per se, but indicated a revival of interest in the Harlem River waterways. Then in 1863 another company, officially named the Hudson and Harlem River Canal Company, was incorporated.[25] The legislature renewed this new company's term in 1866 for three more years.[26]

The Hudson and the Harlem River Canal Company was quiet about the project until 1870 when it was brought into the public eye because of a suit involving the right of way across the property owned by the Hudson River Rolling Mill Company.[27] The action was not, however, to be the Hudson and Harlem River Canal Company's main problem. In 1870 the private charter had expired by limitation and the State Legislature refused renewal, claiming the "it was deemed unwise to subject an arm of the sea to the control of a private corporation."[28]

It seems that the possibilities of a private company undertaking this project were negligible. There were several apparent reasons for this. Not only was there a bias against a private concern having any control over a public access as indicated by the State's refusal to renew the agreement, but it seemed especially difficult for a private concern to deal with the many legal right of way problems involved in the project.

During this period the general belief was the City of New York was going to expand to the north. In 1868 the cross-town streets in Morrisania were given numbers which continued from those which existed in Manhattan.[29] Further:

> By 1869 the State Legislature passed an act, giving the Park Dept. exclusive authority over bridges crossing the Harlem river, and over all streets having an approach thereto.[30]

On January 1, 1874, the areas west of the Bronx River comprising the towns of Morrisania, West Farms and Kingsbridge were annexed to the City of New York. This meant that the City now officially had jurisdiction over the boundaries of the Harlem River and Spuyten Duyvil Creek to the Hudson.[31]

In any case, the Federal Government became involved in the Harlem river area in 1873.[32] Congress ordered a government survey of the area with the objective of constructing a canal in June, 1874.[33] A report was filed by Major General Newton of the U.S. Army Corps of Engineers on February 19, 1874. Basically the report stated that the project was a very worthwhile one:

> Its easy access from the Sound, and moderately easy access from New York Harbor, together with its quiet interior position, would seem to make it a desirable thoroughfare for vessels passing from Long Island Sound to the Hudson River, and, in certain cases, even for those passing between New York Harbor on the East River and the Hudson.[34]

General Newton pointed out that there were may artificial obstructions, in addition to the natural ones, that hindered navigation of the stream. All six bridges across the Harlem were too low and their piers were affecting the flow of water. He recommended that future bridge construction plans be approved by Congress. In further reports written in 1875, 1876, and 1881 Newton outlined the optimal procedure for straightening the Spuyten Duyvil Creek connection between the Harlem and the Hudson Rivers.[35] *The New York Times* reported on General Newton's survey in March of 1874 and indicted that the operations would be "somewhat tedious and expensive."[36]

But Congress made its first appropriation for the scheme in 1875 at the request of the New York State Legislature.[37] In 1877 Congressman Benjamin A. Willis was instrumental in procuring another appropriation.[38]

These appropriations, however, were not to result in commencing work, for there were still many problems with the right of way. In 1878 Newton recommended to General Humphreys, the Chief of Engineers, that the owners of the property along the canal route not be compensated for right of way. Newton felt that the owners were holding out for more money, and as long as there was a chance of their receiving some they would continue to hold out. He suggested that the Government:

> . . . hold firm in the refusal to pay anything for the right of way, and if improvement of the Harlem be not of sufficient moment to the great State and City of New York to insure a gift of right of way, then let it go by default.[39]

A commission was set up by the Supreme Court of New York State to assess the potential damages and benefits to property owners along the proposed canal route.[40] In 1881 the *New York Tribune* reported that progress was being made "by slow degrees," and the hope was to complete the project by 1883 at a cost of two million dollars. Unfortunately most of the progress that had been made was in trying to acquire the right of way. The Commission was still investigating the problem at the time, and the *Tribune* further stated:

> If this Commission and those charged with the legal pro-
> ceedings comprehended the injury growing out of tardiness
> on their part they would doubtless by persuaded to con-
> clude their labors, and the press can do nothing more serv-
> iceable to the community than to impress upon them the
> importance of quickly completing their work.[41]

When the Commission finally filed their report in early 1883, they awarded the property owners compensation for damages and presented a schedule for each award, which filled two large volumes. *The New York Times* reported: "The total amount of the estimated benefits which will result from the improvement is $258,892, and of the damages for which compensation is to be allowed, if the report is confirmed, $147,813."[42]

The Commissioners that issued the report, General William Smith, and Messrs. William Grace and James Fish, presented a bill for their effort amounting to $110,000. Their billing received almost as much attention as the compensation to the property owners. Indeed there seemed to be more objection to it. The main contention was that the Commissioners were already compensated in their respective positions and were entitled only to expenses incurred.[43] Ultimately they received their compensation as they showed that their work involved an extreme-ly difficult case which included attendance at over six hundred meetings and the coverage of fourteen square miles of assessment.[44]

The estimated cost at this point for cutting the connection through Dyckman's meadows (today the area under and around the Broadway Bridge) based on General Newton's 1882 survey was $2,100,000. In addi-tion improvements of the Harlem River itself to its mouth would cost another $600,000; thus the total project was to cost $2,700,000. Congress had appropriated funds of $400,000, but that was contingent on secur-ing the right of way free of cost according to the River and Harbor Acts of 1878 and 1879.[45]

A New York State Law of April 22, 1876, had authorized the United States Government to "take and hold as much land, and land under water, for any improvements thereon, as may be necessary for the locations, construction and convenient use of the said improvement." It had also restricted the line of the cut to be made to the Spuyten Duyvil Creek. General Newton had shown, however, that the cut should be made straight through Dyckman's Meadow to the Hudson. Thus the law had to be amended, and it was on May 20, 1879.[46]

The executors of the Ogden estate were, however, dissatisfied with the $6,700 award granted by the Commission and demanded a change in the adopted boundary lines of the project so as to avoid their property.[47] This issue was brought to court and further delayed the project. The matter was finally settled by the United States Attorney General, A.H. Garland who refused the Ogden estate appeal on the grounds that the land was granted to the United States Government under the April 22, 1876, and May 20, 1879, Laws of the State of New York.

The actual right of way and needed land were turned over to the Federal Government as soon as the *Report of the Commissioners of Estimate and Assessment* was entered in the Office of the Clerk of the City of New York on July 10, 1886. In a letter of May 3, 1887, to the Secretary of War, Attorney General Garland wrote that "the right of way is now fully and completely secured to the United States" and such possession could not be affected by any appeal.[48] The legal action ended, and the Ogden Estate had to accept the Commission's decision.

In 1887 the State conveyed the deed of the land to the United States Government after the commission's estimate of the damage was determined and the City paid or offered to pay the same. Thus the legal difficulties were resolved sufficiently to allow the Congressional appropriations to be released and the work to begin.[49] It took thirteen years, from 1874 to 1887, for this step to be made, and that was with the support of City, State and Federal governmental agencies.

Lieutenant Colonel McFarland pointed out in the 1887 Annual Report of the U.S. Army Chief of Engineers that the:

> . . . legal obstacles which for many years have stood in the way of beginning the work of connecting the Harlem and the Hudson rivers are now removed and the work is about to be begun.[50]

It is no wonder that private companies were stymied in their efforts. In addition to dealing with the individual property owners for the right of way and acquisition of land, the private companies had to contend with governmental departments as well.

With these right of way disputes settled, the project was finally begun in January 1888 under the leadership of Colonel McFarland. It was estimated that the project would take two years to complete.[51] The aim was to:

> . . . dredge a 400 foot wide channel ranging from 15 to 18 feet deep in the Harlem River and to cut through rock in

Dyckman's Meadows to provide a straight channel for Spuyten Duyvil Creek.[52]

At that time, according to a *Scientific American* report, the first "borings were made across the route to determine the character of the soil, and work shortly thereafter began and is now in actual progress."[53] After years of legal battle, the problems now became physical ones. The contract for the cut was awarded to John Satterlee. He encountered some unusual problems, not the least of which was the weather. One of the first steps was to build a coffer dam to prevent water from overflowing into the construction area. This dam was composed of sheet pilings covered with marsh turf taken from the rights of way. As work progressed, the dam, because of the soft mud foundation, gave way and pulled the pilings down. Tons of rock had to be imported and eventually a very expensive rock-fill dam was constructed.[54]

To compound these problems, in March 1888 twenty inches of snow fell in the Great Blizzard of '88. The wind drove the water over the dam and into the cut, leaving a narrow lake instead of a dry canal. The pumps were frozen and flooded and work was further delayed.[55] Then there was the bedrock that had to be cut and blasted through. A *New York Sun* article described the scene in 1890:

> The visitor who approaches the canal along the old Kingsbridge Road, on the east, sees first a great collection of pile drivers, derricks, and other machines for lifting rock, apparently in the middle of the road. When he reaches the spot he finds that the road has been deflected toward the river, where it crosses the proposed canal on the summit of an immense coffer dam . . . Walking in toward the cut the visitor suddenly finds himself facing a gap in the hill 350 feet wide. Rocky walls rise on either side perpendicularly to a height over a hundred feet, their outlines being fringed with great trees. He finds himself standing on the edge of a huge rectangular hole in the solid rock . . . It reminds him of the cellar of a Titan's palace, it is so big and deep.[56]

Masses of rock still had to be removed by the scores of laborers who drilled holes into the solid rocks for blasting.[57]

By 1890 the project was still far from completion. The *New York Telegram* reported that $500,000 would be expended on the cut through Dyckman's Meadow by June 1891. With the unforeseen difficulties the contractors had encountered there was little hope of their completing within schedule.[58]

The *New York Sun* had also reported that since progress on the canal was slow public interest was not lively.[59] That situation was to change very quickly; there arose a host of people who completely objected to the canal. Thus after settling the thorny legal problems and wrestling with the forces of nature, the builders and supporters of the project had to overcome a new onslaught.

The railroads were among the loudest objectors. Representative Ashbel P. Fish was notified by four members of Congress from Connecticut that the River and Harbor Committee had to desist in granting an appropriation to the project until the plans were changed "to meet the approval of the eastern people who travel across the Harlem River."[60] In July 1890 the New-York Mercantile Exchange declared that:

> . . . the canal will, as projected, greatly interfere with the commerce between the upper and lower parts of the Island, other portions of the State and the Eastern States.[61]

The Mercantile Exchange held that the canal should not be open unless provisions were made for the "uninterrupted transit of passengers and goods across the canals on proper bridges."[62]

On the other side of the issue the House Committee on Rivers and Harbors heard testimony in favor of the project in March 1890. Representative Flower claimed that four hundred thousand people of New York lived above the proposed canal and that:

> It should properly be used largely by the canal boats and barges which come down the Erie Canal and obstructed and confused the navigation of the harbor.[63]

A Congressional sub-committee of the River and Harbor Committee came to investigate the site because of the objections that had been raised. The aim was to settle the question whether the work should continue, and, if so, whether the canal should be built for large ships or for lighter craft. The committee was met by a crowd of people who had vested interests on both sides of the issue. The New York Central Railroad representative, Frank Lommas, was against the canal. In addition there were many enthusiastic local supporters of the project, including Fordham Morris.[64] Apparently the sub-committee's report was negative. On August 6, 1890, the *New York Times* reported that $350,000 fro the improvement of the Harlem River had been stricken from the River and Harbor Bill by the Senate Committee.[65]

This action prompted Controller Myers of New York to write a letter to Chairman Frey of the Senate Committee on Commerce. In his letter Myers traced the background of the project. Beginning with the fact that:

> Relying on the good faith of the Government of the Untied States to carry out this work the Legislature of the State of New York authorized proceedings to take forcibly from private owners the necessary lands for it, and to compel riparian owners to pay for these lands and the expenses of acquiring them.[66]

Myers went on to say that the sum of $225,639.95 was paid to the riparian owners and the title acquired by the city has been transferred to the Unites States. The United States Government had begun the work and expended $400,000 toward it. Myers continued:

From the above it will be observed that the faith of the
United States, of the State of New York, and that of the City
of New York are pledged to the execution of this work.[67]

Further, Myers claimed, the project had been before the public for
more than twenty years and was thoroughly discussed in hearings, and it
had received the "sanction of the ablest engineers and the approval of the
whole community." Upon the recommendation of the United States government engineers, comprehensive plans and soundings were done and
the work had commenced:

... and is well underway, then it is now suddenly assailed in
the last stage of progress by unfriendly influences and the
most deeply regrettable delay ensues.[68]

After briefly describing the benefits of the canal, Myers concluded:

The faith of the United States is pledged to the completion
of the work and the necessities of the railroad travel and
traffic crossing the river already provided for by the United
States engineers may with entire propriety and safety be left
to the municipal and State authorities.[69]

Eventually bridges would satisfy the railroad problems and appropriations were continued. The next proposal, however, was to fill in the
canal area and literally connect the island of Manhattan with the mainland. The reasoning was that this would facilitate communication, as it
was claimed that:

... the greatest internal need of the city is facility and speed
of communication between its lower and upper parts, and
the utmost ease of expansion and movement for its population.[70]

The Harlem River was thus considered a serious obstruction and the
canal would only make matters worse by further cutting Manhattan off
from the mainland. The suggestion was that, if the river could not be
filled in with its area turned into real estate, then:

It should be bridged at every point where it is desirable to
cross it by railroad or highway, every bridge should be at
level most convenient for transit, and none of them should
be broken by "draws."[71]

In a quite serous proposal, Simon Stevens, a lawyer, presented to the
Mayor of New York on January 20, 1892, a plan to fill in the Harlem
River. Stevens gave a history of the canal project and claimed that the
canal scheme had been:

... dangling in the air for the past seventeen years, and there
is not the slightest probability that in any event it can be
completed in the ensuing six years.[72]

He further asserted that the canal if completed:

... would never be anything more than a nuisance to be

cursed by nineteen-twentieths of the people who reside in
or who visit New York from above the Harlem River.[73]

Stevens maintained that $8,500,000 would be saved on the canal, the
bridges, and other waterfront improvements, if the area were filled in. He
felt that the new land would be worth ten million dollars for tax purpos-
es. Detailed plans were submitted to substantiate his proposal, Stevens
contended:

> . . . the march of improvement on the upper end of
> Manhattan Island has been so stupendous that there has
> developed a great necessity for practically closing to naviga-
> tion that part of the Harlem River between Third and
> Eighth Avenues [in The Bronx from Third Avenue to 165th
> Street], by filling it in between these points, leaving only a
> covered water way, 60 feet wide, to be built on the westerly
> side of the river at a height of not less than 7 feet above
> mean high water of spring tides, and extending the avenues
> and streets of Harlem into Morrisania.[74]

Mayor Hugh Grant "scoffed" at the proposal and said:

> I am absolutely opposed to any such scheme. I will always
> vote against it. You know, Mr. Stevens, it is in the interest of
> the railroads . . . Why doesn't Paris fill in the Seine, London
> the Thames, New-York the North River: . . I don't think this
> matter worth an argument.[75]

Fordham Morris, a leading proponent of the canal project, denounced
the filling-in scheme, and the New York Central for supporting it. The
New York Times in reporting Morris's position also claimed that:

> The "Vanderbilt system" [New York Central Railroad] has
> been for many years so managed as to ensure the warm detes-
> tation of everybody whose interests are in any way dependent
> upon it.[76]

The issue was debated throughout 1892 and even into 1893. On
February 1, 1893, *The New York Times* contained an editorial in support
of filling in the area and claimed that the canal project "exists simply as
an obstruction to the settlement of the purely local question raised by the
existence of the Harlem River."[77]

This article was one of the few newspaper reports that viewed the
canal negatively. It continued:

> Until the Harlem is filled up, or reduced to its lowest terms
> as a water course, the expansion of New York is interrupted.
> It is too bad that this city should be put to a useless and con-
> tinuing inconvenience because somebody fancies that at
> some time the navigability of the Harlem may be important
> to the Nation at large.[78]

Despite this opposition the work continued.[79]

Originally the canal was designed to connect the Hudson River and the Dyckman's Meadow cut with a nearly straight channel. This, however, involved cutting though a valuable peninsula where the Johnson Iron Foundry was located.[80] The high property value obviously forced the Army Corps of Engineers to avoid the foundry by leaving in the bell-shaped bend to its south. By 1879 it was decided that after Dyckman's Meadow the proposed line would follow as "nearly as possible" the course of the Spuyten Duyvil to the Hudson River.[81]

The canal, by July of 1893, extended from the mouth of the Spuyten Duyvil Creek to the site called the Bell Pumpkin Meadow, near the Hudson River. While most of the work involved the cut through Dyckman's Meadow, which was enclosed by a dam at each end, the area from the Bell Pumpkin Meadow to the Spuyten Duyvil Creek was cut and dredged to within 140 feet of the west dam. This was "as close as it was deemed advisable with safety to dredge at the time,"[82]

By 1895 the canal was finally navigable, though not complete. The ceremonies for opening day were debated with the usual squabbling that characterized the project from its start. The committee in charge of the opening celebrations was as complex as the project itself, and included Federal, State, City and local representatives. Fordham Morris was asked to be the orator, and, after some debate, ex-Mayor Abram S. Hewitt was asked to make a speech along with Major William L. Strong and other dignitaries. Two parades, one on land and the other in the water, were coordinated. Elaborate displays of fireworks were arranged at a couple of sites. Oak Point in The Bronx was the general headquarters for the celebration.[83] At noon the cruiser *Cincinnati* in the Hudson River fired a salvo and with a parade of vessels entered the new canal and steamed down the Harlem River with many thousands lining the route.[84]

The day included a banquet at Oak Point with the general public invited. *The New York Times* reported:

> The new waterway, destined to be of such great advantage to the commerce of the Hudson, was subjected a severe test of its practical commercial advantages, and it was proved beyond question that it is, even in its present shape, safe and easy of navigation under all circumstances. The canal saves over twenty-five miles of distance in the traffic between the Hudson and Long Island Sound.[85]

In his address at the banquet at Oak Point, Fordham Morris traced the history of the area back to Henry Hudson's anchoring of the *Half Moon* off Spuyten Duyvil in 1609. Morris, whose father, Lewis G. Morris, led the farmers who tore down Macomb's bridge in 1838, said:

> Our fathers were seafaring men, and the great river and lake systems were the highways of commerce from earliest times. Steam had wrought its changes; but today the canal boat carries as much grain as ten carloads on the railways, and

the schooner and barge are friendly rivals or adjuncts of the railways.[86]

Morris praised Lieutenant Colonel Gillespie (General Newton had since died) and the Army Corps of Engineers and his staff for the work. He reported that no life had been lost through "flood, tempest and other untoward circumstances [that] have surrounded the enterprise."[87]

At the 1895 opening the canal was not completely dredged. *Engineering News* stated at the time that calling the canal a "ship canal" was "somewhat misleading." The canal was about ten feet deep at mean low water level and one hundred and forty to one hundred and sixty feet wide.[88]

Since the full plan called for a canal four hundred feet wide and fifteen feet deep at low tide, the project was far from finished. Morris warned: "Do not forget that $1,750,000 is still required to finish this work."[89]

Not everyone was as delighted as Morris and the other celebrants on opening day. Charles B. Stoughton, a wealthy resident of Morrisania, was greatly dissatisfied with the canal's progress. For many years he had envisioned connecting the Hudson to Long Island Sound. Historian Randall Comfort reported in 1906 that Stoughton put his vision into action as early as 1876:

> Pursuing this idea, on the twelfth of October, 1876, he called
> a meeting of the citizens at his home, and issued a missive,
> expressing the essential proposition which he was to ampli-
> fy in subsequent papers.[90]

Stoughton dreamed of making Port Morris the central point in New York City leading to the rest of the world by ship and railway.[91] He offered to construct the Harlem River canal and furnish the right of way for $1,000,000 less than the sum estimated by General Newton.[92] The canal Stoughton proposed was to be three hundred feet wide. A resolution was even introduced in Congress to contract Stoughton to do the work.[93] Stoughton, however, did not receive the contract.

After the opening of the canal in 1895 Stoughton wrote a letter to Congress describing the seventy years of legislation surrounding the canal project. He decried the fact that his original proposal was not considered and claimed that he could have done a better job, in less time, and at almost half the price. He claimed, further, that the project was not done in a "workmanlike manner."[94] Although Stoughton never got a contract, he apparently was instrumental in getting the support of Congress and of commercial interests to get the canal completed. Fordham Morris praise Stoughton in his 1895 address:

> Many have advocated this scheme, but no one deserves
> more credit than our specially designated guest, Mr. Charles
> Stoughton, whom we are pleased to see with us today. To his
> efforts before Congress and in the various commercial

exchanges of other State, we owe that outside support without which this enterprise might have failed.[95]

In 1895 the Harlem River Canal project was already sixty-nine years in the making. It still had forth-three more years to go before it would be completed. But its progress toward the final goal was to be slow and the struggle focused on man-made obstructions.

In 1906 the North Side Board of Trade submitted a statement to the House Committee on Rivers and Harbors calling for an appropriation for the completion of the Harlem Ship Canal. At the time more than sixty percent of the work had been completed with the total appropriations of $1,416,000. The Board claimed that $1,305,000 was required to finish the project, and that amount was "less than one half of one percent of $270,000,000, the value of the tonnage carried on the Harlem Ship Canal during the year 1905." The appropriations in the past had averaged $41,600 per year, so the Board estimated that, if that rate was to continue, "it would require thirty-one years longer to complete the improvement."[96] Ironically their forecast about the completion time was exactly on target.

The argument of the Board of Trade was based on several factors which favored the completion of the canal. It was, of course, part of New York Harbor, "the greatest shipping Port of the world." Thus the project was in the "commercial, agricultural and manufacturing interests of the whole country." It was important because:

> . . . upon the peaceful waters of that stream there is now carried by the swift steamer, the three masted schooner and by the commodious lighter, canal boat and barge the products of the forest, the field, and the mine and the factory amounting in round number to Ten Millions of tons and valued at over Two Hundred and Seventy Millions of Dollar.[97]

In addition, the Board's statement claimed the project should be completed because it was an essential part of the New York State Canal system, "that great continuous and free water way extending from Duluth to the Atlantic."[98] since the project had begun, nearly a million people had settled around the stream and businesses had been set up around it.

> Situated as it is in the center of this great population, the most rapidly growing community in the Untied States, it is the natural carrier for the provisions that feed these people, for the lumber, the iron, the stone, the brick, the lime and other materials that enter into their vast building operations, and for the fuel that heats and lights their homes and places of employment and produces that power that turns the wheels of their busy industries and propels their elevated, surface and underground railway cars. The docks of this stream are the storage and distributing depots of the bulky merchandise that enter in the daily life and activities of this large and enterprising community.[99]

View west across Spuyten Duyvil Creek, c. 1900.
A mounted policeman can be seen in center, on Johnson Avenue above the
retaining wall. The house in the creek is on an island accessible by foot bridge.
The area is now in the vicinity of Kennedy High School.
The Bronx County Historical Society Research Library.

The Harlem River Ship Canal, by its very existence even in unfinished form, had become extremely important to the life blood of the City. The canal was now its own best argument for its completion.

The 1909 *Report* of the United States Army Chief of Engineers indicated that work was progressing, and called for an appropriation of $300,000 to continue work through 1911.[100]

Then in 1913 a new issue emerged. A change of the route of the canal was proposed. The problem was the sharp bend in the canal near the junction with the Hudson River. It was claimed that:

> . . . even short boats find it difficult to make this sharp turn, without bumping into the banks.[101]

In June 1913 Congressman Joseph A. Goulden of New York City introduced a bill in the House of Representatives requesting an appropriation of $850,000 to straighten the bend which involved the curve near the Johnson Iron Foundry.[102] The issue was still unresolved in 1918 when a conference was held by the Bronx Board of Trade to devise a scheme that would eliminate the bend. One plan involved a right of way through the property owned by the Johnson Iron Works.[103]

At a conference for Federal State and City engineers it was deemed that the City had to take the initiative. During that meeting an additional problem was brought out; that of the obstruction of the High Bridge.[104] In April 1918 consulting engineer Louis Haffen (a former Bronx Borough President) suggested a new plan that involved exchanging two hundred feet of the Johnson Iron Works property for underwater land. Haffen explained: " . . .destruction of the Johnson plant is out of the question at the present time."[105]

By 1923 apparently the time was right because the Johnson Iron Works were closed by a decision of the State Supreme Court. According to the 1923 article in *Iron Age* magazine, the property:

> . . . jutting out into the Harlem River at Spuyten Duyvil, was condemned for the purpose of removal to widen the channel of the river as provided by Congress and the State Legislature.

The peninsula was to be released to the State by July 1, 1923, "for wrecking or whatever method of disposal decided upon by public authorities."[106]

Thus one factor that stood in the way of opening the Harlem River to deep water traffic was removed. The other factor was the High Bridge, some of whose piers interfered with the tidal flow of the Harlem River making navigation difficult.[107] The problem was the closeness of its graceful arches. The arches restricted the movement of ships and caused dangerous currents. Although no longer the sole conveyer of water in the Croton aqueduct system, the High Bridge by this time had gained status as an historic structure, so there was much resistance to its destruction. A Board which convened on this issue in June of 1919, nevertheless, claimed that it was "lovely but useless" and so advocated its abandonment "for the greater benefit of the city."[108] In September 1919 at a public hearing towing companies contended that the bridge should be completely removed. Local groups from Washington Heights and The Bronx objected, however, even to removing some pillars from under the bridge.[109]

A *Scientific American* article in May 1920 suggested that some piers of the High Bridge be removed from the channel in this way:

> . . . spanning the gap by a flat arch, which will be built of re-enforced concrete and faced with stone recovered from the old work. Thus will a beautiful and historic work be preserved to the city.[110]

Ultimately a plan along these lines was adopted. In 1928-29 five of the larger arches were removed and a single steel arch was substituted.[111]

By 1938 the work on the Ship Canal was virtually compete. A channel fifteen feet deep at low water level and four hundred feet wide had been excavated from the East River to the High Bridge. Between the High Bridge and the Hudson River the canal was fifteen feet deep but 350 feet wide. Some minor work remained which included additional dredging above the High Bridge and the completion of the straightening of the channel around the old Johnson Iron Works site.[112]

Thus the one hundred and twelve year old project quietly wound to a close, with no fanfare, no parades and no fireworks. In the intervening time, the surrounding area had developed as expected. In 1937 Erwin Crane wrote in *Bronxboro* magazine The Bronx was:

> . . . steadily growing in the direction of a distribution terminal. Indeed, it is ideally located for such a terminal. It is the only borough of the five on the mainland.
>
> . . . tributary waters are essential to the growth of a community into a point of distribution. Thus, we have the Harlem River, bounding The Bronx on the west and comprising a connecting link between the Hudson River, and the Long Island Sound. Through this channel, vessels come from New England and up through lower New York bay bound for upper stretches of New York through the barge canal system of the state.[113]

A canal linking the Hudson and Harlem Rivers was a good idea from the very first. Some good ideas take time to succeed. So it was with the Harlem River Ship Canal.

Aerial view, looking west, of the Canal in 1937. In the center
of the channel, the Johnson Iron Works peninsula excavation is
shown underway. Columbia University's Baker Field is in the
center, above and to the left of the Broadway Bridge.
Note that the Henry Hudson Bridge has only one deck.
Courtesy of The Riverdale Press and Rev. William Tieck.

NOTES

[1] *The New York Times*, February 1,1893, p. 4, col. 2.

[2] Charles B. Stoughton, *"Harlem River and Kills Canal: 70 Years Legislation."* Letter to U.S. Congress, May 10, 1897, New-York Historical Society; see also James L. Wells, *North Side Board of Trade Statement in Favor of an Appropriation for the Completion of the Harlem Ship Canal, Submitted to the House of Representatives Committee on Rivers and Harbors*, Washington, D.C., December 15, 1905 (New York: North Side Board of Trade, 1907), p. 4.

[3] Stephen Jenkins, *The Story of The Bronx 1639-1912* (New York: G.P. Putnam's Sons, 1912), pp. 188, 196, 207, 331. North Side Board of Trade, *The Great North Side or Borough of The Bronx* (New York: Knickerbocker Press, 1897), pp. 62-65.

[4] Susan Elizabeth Lyman, *The Story of New York* (New York: Crown Publishers, Inc., 1964). pp. 5, 202-3.

[5] J. Thomas Scharf, *History of Westchester County, New York, Including Morrisania, Kingsbridge, and West Farms*, 2 Vols. (Philadelphia: L.E. Preston and Co., 1886).

[6] Noble E. Whitford, *History of the Barge Canal of New York State*, New York State Engineer's Supplement to the Annual Report of the State Engineer and Surveyor (State of New York, June 30, 1921), p. 437.

[7] "The Harlem River Improvement and Ship Canal," *Scientific American*, Supplement No. 1015, June 15, 1895.

[8] Harlem River and Spuyten Duyvil Association, *Report on the Origin and Present Condition of the Improvement with Some Suggestions as to the Drawbridge Question and the Commercial Interests Affected Thereby* (New York: n.p., 1893), New-York Historical Society.

[9] Fordham Morris, *Address Delivered at the Banquet in the Pavilion at Oak Point on the Occasion of the Opening of the Harlem Ship Canal, June 17, 1895* (New York: North Side Board of Trade, 1896), p. 5.

[10] John McNamara, *History in Asphalt: The Origin of Bronx Street and Place Names Encyclopedia* (New York: The Bronx County Historical Society and Harbor Hill Books, 1978), p. 232.

[11] Reginald Pelham Bolton, *Washington Heights: Its Eventful Past* (New York: Dyckman Institute, 1924), p. 206.

[12] John McNamara, *"Spuyten Duyvil Creek Rich in Ancient Lore,"* *Bronx Press Review*, July 9, 1959.

[13] Whitford, *History of the Barge Canal*, p. 438.

[14] Harlem River and Spuyten Duyvil Association, *Report*, 1893, p. 25.

[15] *Ibid.*, p.26.

[16] Whitford, *History of the Barge Canal*, p. 438.

[17] Laws of the State of New York, April 18, 1826, Chapter 357. See I.N. Phelps Stokes, *Iconography of Manhattan Island, 1492-1909*, Vol. 5, (Republished, New York: Arno Press, 1967), p. 1657.

[18] Laws of the State of New York, April 1827, Chapters 319, 225.

[19] City of New York Common Council Minutes 1784-1831, Vol. 17, January 2, 1827 to February 25, 1828 (New York: City of New York, 1917), p. 387.

[20] Morris, *Address*, p. 7.

[21] "The Hudson and Harlem River Canal Project," *Commercial and Financial Chronicle*, August , 1870, p. 165.

[22] Harlem River and Spuyten Duyvil Association, *Report*, 1893, p. 26.

[23] Morris, *Address*, p. 7.

[24] Stokes, *Iconography*, Vol. 5, p. 1889.

[25] Laws of the State of New York, May 2, 1863, Chapter 365.

[26] Laws of the State of New York, April 10, 1866, Chapter 494.

[27] "The Hudson and Harlem River Canal Project," *Commercial and Financial Chronicle, August 6, 1870*, p. 166.

[28]Harlem River and Spuyten Duyvil Association, *Report*, 1893, p. 26; see also, Morris, Address, p. 8.

[29]North Side Board of Trade, *The Great North Side*, p. 22.

[30]*Ibid.*

[31]*Ibid.*, p. 19.

[32]United States Army Annual Report of the Chief of Engineers 1887 (Washington D.C.: U.S. Army, 1887), p. 666.

[33]*Ibid.*

[34]United State Army Annual Report of the Chief of Engineers 1874, p. 169.

[35]Marion J. Kalwonn, *Cradle of the Corps: A History of the New York District U.S. Army Corps of Engineers 1775-1975* (New York: U.S. Army, 1977), p. 103.

[36]"The Harlem River," *The New York Times*, March 17, 1874, p. 1, col. 4.

[37]Laws of the State of New York, 1875, Chapter 816.

[38]"Improving the Harlem," *New York Tribune*, January 31, 1881, p. 3, col. 1.

[39]"Improvement of the Harlem," *New York Tribune*, January 31, 1879, p. 5, col 4.

[40]"The Harlem River Canal," *The New York Times*, February 16, 1880, p. 5, col 1.

[41]"Improving the Harlem," *New York Tribune*, January 31, 1881, p. 3, col 1.

[42]"The Harlem River Canal," *The New York Times*, March 7, 1883, p. 3, col. 2.

[43]"Harlem Ship Canal Bills,: *The New York Times*, April 20, 1883, p. 3, col. 3.

[44]"Believing the Charges Moderate," *The New York Times*, February 20, 1885, p. 20, col. 4; "James D. Fish Allowed $6,000," *The New York Times*, June 30, 1885, p. 8, col. 2.

[45]United States Army, *Annual Report of Chief of Engineers 1887*, pp. 668-9.

[46]*Ibid.*

[47]"The Harlem River Canal," *The New York Times*, March 7, 1883, p. 3, col.2.

[48]United States Army, *Annual Report of Chief of Engineers*, 1887, pp. 673-5.

[49]*Ibid.*, pp. 674-5.

[50]*Ibid.*, pp. 665-6.

[51]"Harlem River Ship Canal," *Engineering News and Contract Journal, May 21, 1887*, p. 339.

[52]Kalwonn, *Cradle of the Corps*, p. 103.

[53]"Harlem River Improvement and Ship Canal," *Scientific American*, March 22, 1890, p. 183.

[54]Kalwonn, *Cradle of the Corps*, pp. 103-4

[55]*Ibid.*, pp. 104-5.

[56]"The Harlem Ship Canal," *New York Sun*, 1890, New-York Historical Society.

[57]*bid.*

[58]"Cash for the Channels," *New York Telegram*, March 8, 1890, p. 1.

[59]"The Harlem Ship Canal," *New York Sun*, 1890.

[60]"The Harlem Ship Canal," *The New York Times*, March 8, 1890, p. 8, col. 3.

[61]"The Harlem Ship Canal," *The New York Times*, July 11, 1890, p. 2, col. 2.

[62]*Ibid.*

[63]"The Harlem Ship Canal," *The New York Times*, March 15, 1890, p. 5, col. 5.

[64]"The Harlem River Canal," *The New York Times*, April 1, 1890, p. 8, col. 2.

[65]"Harlem River Improvement," *The New York Times*, August 6, 1890, p.8, col. 7.

[66]*Ibid.*

[67]*Ibid.*

[68]*Ibid.*

[69]*Ibid.*

[70]"The Harlem River Question," *The New York Times*, February 8, 1891, p. 4, col. 3.

[71]*Ibid.*, p. 4, col 4.

[72]Simon Stevens, "The Harlem River Ship Canal," Letter from, December 25, 1891, p. 9, New-York Historical Society.

[73]*Ibid.*

[74]*Ibid.*, p. 4.

[75]"The Mayor Scoffs at It," *The New York Times*, March 3, 1892, p. 5, col. 5.

[76]"The Central and The Harlem," *The New York Times*, July 20, 1892, p.4, col. 3.

[77]*The New York Times*, February 1, 1893, p. 4, col. 2.

[78]*Ibid.*

[79]In 1891 workers found mastodon remains during the excavation. The remains were embedded in the peat sixteen feet below the low water level. Lieutenant Colonel Gillespie, who was then in charge of the project, presented the findings to the American Museum of Natural History; see Stokes, *Iconography*, vol. 5, pp. 2006-7.

[80]William A. Tieck, *Riverdale, Kingsbridge, Spuyten Duyvil* (Old Tappan, New Jersey: Fleming H. Revell Co: 1968), p. 137.

[81]United States Army, *Annual Report of Chief of Engineers, 1889*, p. 768.

[82]"Locked in Gen. Casey's Desk," *The New York Times*, July 28, 1893, p. 9, col. 3.

[83]"The Harlem Ship Canal," *The New York Times*, May 11, 1895, p.8, col. 3.

[84]Tieck, *Riverdale, Kingsbridge, Spuyten Duyvil*, pp. 137-8

[85]"Hudson Weds the Sound," *The New York Times*, June 18, 1895, p. 1, col. 8.

[86]Morris, *Address*, pp. 6, 10.

[87]*Ibid.*, p. 9.

[88]"The Harlem River Ship Canal," *Engineering News and American Railway Journal, June 20, 1895*, p. 399.

[89]Morris, *Address*, p. 10.

[90]Randall Comfort, *History of Bronx Borough* (New York: North Side News Press, 1906), p. 277.

[91]*Ibid.*

[92]"The Harlem River Canal," *Engineering News and American Contract Journal, February, 10, 1883*, p. 71.

[93]"The Harlem River Canal," *The New York Times*, January 6, 1882, p.1 , col. 3.

[94]Stoughton, "Harlem River and Kills Canals: 70 Years Legislation."

[95]Morris, *Address*, p. 8.

[96]Wells, *North Side Board of Trade Statement*, p. 8.

[97]*Ibid.*, p. 16.

[98]*Ibid.*

[99]*Ibid.*, p. 17.

[100]United States Army, *Annual Report of Chief of Engineers 1908-9*, pp. 1071-2.

[101]"Plan New Route for Harlem Ship Canal," *The New York Times*, March 21, 1913, p. 17, col. 1.

[102] "Improving Waterfront," *The New York Times*, June 1, 1913, p. 1, col. 2.

[103]"Harlem River Channel: *The New York Times*, January 13, 1918, p. 8, col. 7.

[104]"Discuss Harlem River Improvement," *The New York Times*, January 27, 1918, p. 8, col. 1.

[105]"Harlem River Widening," *The New York Times*, April 7, 1918, p. 10, col. 5.

[106]"*Iron Age*," June 21, 1923, p. 1773.

[107]"Influence of Harlem River," *Industrial Management, May 1919*, p. 356.

[108]"Plans to Improve Harlem River," *The New York Times*, June 29, 1919, p. 9, col. 2.

[109]"To Widen Harlem Channel," *The New York Times*, September 9, 1919, p. 24, col. 3.

[110] "Opening Up the Harlem River," *Scientific American*, May 8, 1920, p. 507.

[111]Roger Arcara, "The Bronx-Then and Now: The High Bridge," *The Bronx Country Historical Society Journal*, January 1971, p. 38.

[112]"Improvement of Waterways," *Bronxboro*, February-March, 1938, p. 6.

[113]Erwin Crane, "Inland Bronx Waterways," *Bronxboro*, June, 1937, pp. 3, 4, 9.

Special thanks to researcher Jay Filan.

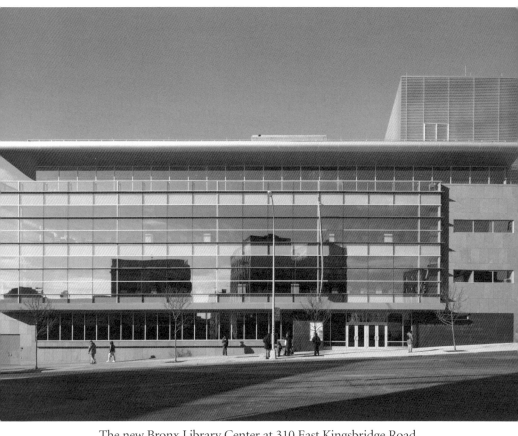

The new Bronx Library Center at 310 East Kingsbridge Road.
Courtesy of The New York Public Library.

8.

Historical Research in a Library

**University, Municipal, Historical Society,
Business, or other Libraries
afford great opportunities for research.**

A library's general collection of books, periodicals, atlases and vertical files, can be searched utilizing a computer, as most large libraries have computerized their catalogue or in the card catalogue where it is still in use.

With very few exceptions, the following reference books are in most research libraries. The list is selective as there are many other valuable reference materials in the library in addition to these. Always ask the librarian for assistance as they are trained to assist you.

HISTORICAL RESEARCH IN A UNIVERSITY OR HISTORICAL SOCIETY LIBRARY

References

1. Guides to Books and Periodicals by Subject:

Balay, Robert. *Guide to Reference Books.* 11th ed., Chicago: American Library Assn., 1996.

This is a guide to guides. It is the librarian's bible, the single most useful tool when you want to know where to turn to find something. Is there an atlas for South Africa? Is there a Puerto Rican encyclopedia? This guide is the place to go to find out.

Besterman, Theodore. *A World Bibliography of Bibliographies.* 4th ed., Lausanne, Switzerland: Societas Bibliographia, 1965-67.

A very valuable list of bibliographies on historical topics, many of them highly specialized and/or obscure.

Subject Guide to Books in Print. New Providence, NJ: Bowker, 2004.

2. Indices to Historical Writings:

American Economic Association, *Index of Economic Journals.* Illinois: M. R. Irwin, to 2003.

Excellent for economic history.

Norton, Mary Beth. *Guide to Historical Literature.* New York: Oxford University Press, 1995.

Published for the American Historical Association.

It is very valuable as a general bibliographical guide to the "classics" but rapidly gets out of date. Monographs only, but comprehensive to published date.

Coulter, E. M. and Gerstenfeld, M. *Historical Bibliographies.* New York: Russell & Russell, reprint of 1935 ed.

Similar to Norton but older.

Writings on American History. Boston: St. Martin's Press, 2004.

Annual publication issued as Part 2 of the Annual Report of the American Historical Association.

Historical Abstracts. Santa Barbara, CA: ABC-Clio, annual.

Benjamin, Jules. *A Student's Guide to History.* 9th ed., Boston: St. Martin's Press, 2004.

Harvard Guide to American History. Cambridge, MA: Belknap Press, 1974.
Valuable in many ways, especially for annotations.

3. Indices to General Periodical Literature:

Social Sciences and Humanities Index, formerly known as *International Index.*
The most useful general periodical index since it also includes non-American sources since 1907.

Readers Guide to Periodical Literature. New York: H. W. Wilson, since 1900.

Public Affairs Information Service Bulletin-since 1915.
English language materials especially on politics, diplomacy, economics, etc.

Poole's Index to Periodical Literature. New York: A. Smith, 1802-1906.
Contains no foreign language American papers but otherwise is quite comprehensive.

The New York Times Index.
This index is also available on their web site from the beginning of the paper.

4. Encyclopedias:

Encyclopedia Britannica-2004.

Grand Larousse Encyclopedia, ten volumes (1960-1964).
Use general encyclopedias with caution. They are handy but are not adequate as sources of interpretations or analysis. Their value is as a convenient compendia of facts, or as quick surveys of historical questions. Another good place to go for a convenient introduction to a subject is a school textbook. Needless to say, these also are inadequate for serious analysis of a thesis.

The New Schaff-Herzog Encyclopedia of Religious Knowledge. Grand Rapids, MI: Baker, 1949-50.

The New Catholic Encyclopedia. Detroit: Thomas/Gale, 2003.

Encyclopedia of Philosophy. New York: Macmillan, 1967.

Hastings, James. *Encyclopedia of Religion and Ethics.* New York: Scribner, 1924.

McNamara, John. *History in Asphalt: The Origin of Bronx Street & Place Names Encyclopedia.* The Bronx, NY:
The Bronx County Historical Society, 2002 revised edition.

The Encyclopedia of New York City. Yale University Press, 1995.

Encyclopedias exist on every possible subject. Subject encyclopedias are very valuable sources for general information on specialized fields, technical terminology, navigation, magic, arts, astronomy, etc.

5. General Compendia of Historical Facts:

Laner, Wm. L. *An Encyclopedia of World History.*
Boston: Houghton Mifflin, 2001.

Morris, R. B. *An Encyclopedia of American History.*
New York: Harper-Collins, 1996.

6. Statistical Sources:

The Statesmans Yearbook. London: Macmillan, 1971.

The United Nations Yearbook. United Nations Publishing Service, annual.

Statistical Yearbook. United Nations Publishing Service, annual.

Demographic Yearbook. United Nations Publishing Service, annual.

The Statistical Abstracts of the United States, 1878-2004. Census Bureau.

Historical Statistics of the United States, Colonial Times:
A Statistical Abstract Supplement. Census Bureau, 1997

The World Almanac and Book of Facts. New York: World Almanac, 2005.

U. S. Census Reports. Census Bureau.

Abstract of British Historical Statistics. London:
Cambridge University Press, 1971.

European Historical Statistics 1750-1950. London:
Cambridge University Press, 1975.

Facts-on-File, Inc. New York: Facts on File, 2004, annual.

CD-*Roms in Print.* Westport, CT.: Meckler, 1987, annual.

National Data Book. U. S. Department of Commerce, Economics and Statistics Administration, Census Bureau, Washington D. C.

7. Biographical Guides:

There are several one-volume dictionaries of biography. The most useful are the national biographies and encyclopedias. All except *Who's Who* include only deceased persons.

Dictionary of National Biography-Britain. London:
Oxford University Press, 2004.

The National Encyclopedia of American Biography. New York:
T. J. White, 1926-1984.

Dictionary of American Biography. New York: Scribner's, to 1996.

For current biography see: *Who's Who.* New Providence, N. J.:
Marquis, annual.

There is one for the U. S. A., several for regions of the U. S., some for European countries, in English. Also see *Current Biography* which is published by H. W. Wilson & Co.

Who Was Who. New Providence, N. J.: Marquis, annual.
Obituaries of leading citizens.

8. Atlases:

Millennium World Atlas. New York: Rand McNally & Co., 2000.

Commercial Atlas & Marketing Guide. New York: Rand McNally, 2004. Population, economic and geographical data.

Shepherd, William R. *Historical Atlas.* New York: Barnes & Noble, 1962.

The Times Atlas of the World. Comprehensive Edition, London: Times Books, 1999.

The National Atlas of the United States of America. Reston, Virginia: U.S. Coast & Geodetic Survey, annual.

9. Dictionaries:

All sorts of dictionaries exist, from the known to the widely obscure, such as the *Dictionary of American Naval Ships, The Visual Dictionary, The Dictionary of Toys.*

A New English Dictionary on Historical Principles.

Also known as the *Oxford English Dictionary,* this publication is a monument to 19th century scholarship and was published by Oxford University Press. Here was an attempt to give not just the meaning of a word but the history of its meaning, when the word first appeared, and the changes which have occurred in its usage.

There is a good selection of foreign language and English dictionaries shelved in the general reference area.

These guides tell you where a book, periodical, or manuscript material in the United States, can be found.

10. Guides and Union Lists:

Union List of Serials in the Libraries of the U. S. and Canada. New York: H. W. Wilson, since 1924.

This is the most valuable union list as it tells you what is available where.

New Serial Titles. New York: R. Bowker, 1953 - to date.

Lists new serials and periodicals with holdings of titles published since January 1950. Picks up where *The Union List of Serials* ends.

National Union Catalog of Manuscripts Collections. Washington, D. C.: Library of Congress, 1959-current.

Gregory, W. *American Newspapers. 1821-1936,* New York: Krass Reprint Co., 1977.

There are many other union lists and guides.

11. The Internet and Partial Library Collections on the Web.

View of the new computer floor in The Bronx Library Center.
Courtesy of The New York Public Library.

9.

The Internet

How can it be used?

The Internet is a world wide system of connected databases around the globe that allows users to communicate and share files utilizing a computer.

"The Net" has become the largest and fastest information network in history and connects the entire world.

And it is growing!

A BRIEF HISTORY OF
THE INTERNET

The Internet was started back in the early 1960s by the Pentagon's Advanced Research Projects Agency (ARPA) as a research project to develop a means of sharing information on super computers in remote locations. The defense industry, as well as the Rand Corporation, a think tank, saw the potential for connecting military and defense organizations as a guard against the possibility of nuclear attack. If an attack were to occur in a strategic location, then that information would not be lost because it could be accessed via a wire connection by a computer in another location.

With the fall of U.S.S.R. in the late 1980s and early 1990s, interest in the Internet shifted to education. Universities were among the first institutions to explore the potential use of this new form of communicating and information dissemination. At the time, the Internet was used primarily as a means of moving files from one location to another. It required complicated codes and formatting by experts.

In 1991, the first code for the World Wide Web (www) was created at CERN, a Swiss company that claims to be the worlds largest particle physics laboratory. Using this code, programmers could see the potential for combining text, pictures and other media to publish on the Internet. In the same year Marc Andreesen and students from the University of Illinois developed Mosaic, a graphical browser for the web. In 1993 Mosaic became available and within that year, Internet use increased by 341,634%. (Source: http:/ /www.pbs.org/internet/timeline/index.html).

What is the World Wide Web (www)?

The World Wide Web is a part of the much larger Internet. It is a collection of web pages, which consist of text, pictures and other multimedia that are accessed through the application called a browser. This browser allows the user to navigate to and from the different web sites.

What Do You Need to Connect?

In order to access the Internet, you must have a computer, a modem of some type, and an Internet Service Provider (ISP) which provides access to the Internet. Some of the more common ISP connections utilize telephone lines (dial-up, DSL), cable and Wi-Fi (wireless). This connection serves as your pathway to the Internet and once connected you can have access to virtually unlimited web sites and services (e.g., e-mail, newsgroups) that are available on the Internet. One of the most popular ISPs, is America On Line (AOL) which offers web browsing and e-mail together. Other ISPs require the use of different programs to access these facets.

WEB SITE/WEB PAGES

A web site is made up of web pages. For example the web site is the book and the individual pages are the web pages.

BROWSERS

A browser is a software application used to locate and display web pages. Popular browsers include Netscape, Microsoft Internet, Explorer, Mozilla, Firefox and Safari. These are graphical browsers, which means that they can display pictures and include sound and video as well as text.

Browsers are what enable you to access the documents on the World Wide Web. They translate the code that make up web sites and make them visible on your computer screen.

HOW TO ACCESS WEB SITES

The URL, or Uniform Resource Locator, is the address on the web that you are visiting. If someone gives you the address to their web page, they may say it's at http://www.bronxhistoricalsociety.org.

Web sites are accessed by typing the Uniform Reference Locator into the Location box. If you know the URL, you can type it in and then press the Enter key.

LINKS

Usually, web sites will have links to related or similar information to what is listed on their own site. Clicking on the link may bring you closer to the information you seek in other web sites or web pages. For instance, when browsing The Bronx County Historical Society you can also link to the other six major New York City historical institutions web sites, known collectively as The New York History Coalition.

SEARCH ENGINES

When you do not know the URL or need information on a general topic, you search the internet. There are currently millions of web sites on the web. Fortunately, there are a number of excellent search engines to help you find web sites.

A search engine is a program that searches the world wide web for specified keywords and then lists the documents where the keywords were found as links. Although a search engine is really a general class of pro-grams, the term is often used to specifically describe systems like Google, Yahoo and MSN that enable users to search for documents on the World Wide Web.

A search engine has a database of different websites and their respective keywords. These are usually located by a program called a spider that "crawls" or goes through the websites on the World Wide Web one by one. No search engine has all the sites listed on the Internet. That is why its important to check a number of engines.

Most commonly, searches are activated by typing in keywords that describe the documents or subjects of the documents that you are looking for. Note that you should enter phrases, such as "New York" or "high school" as a way of locating a web site on the subject.

For example, if you are looking for information on Morris High School, you can enter "Morris High School" into the search box, and the websites that mention it will be displayed.

If you did not know the name of the school, then you might enter the following words: New York, Bronx High School.

There are many different search engines that can be used. Here are some of the more popular search engines and some general recommendations for using them:

Google (www.google.com). This is the top rated search engine and has a huge number of websites in its database.

Yahoo (www.yahoo.com). This is another type of search engine. Yahoo is also a site that offers a wide range of resources and services, free e-mail and online calendars and maps.

MSN (www.msn.com). The microsoft network also offers a search engine and an Internet portal.

Saving Bookmarks

One of the most important reasons for book marking sites that you visit is that you are able to find the site again and quickly. Be aware that sites come and go and bookmarks and links do become stale over time.

Description of a Web Site

http://www.bronxhistoricalsociety.org/bookstore//lifeinthebronx.html

http = hypertext transfer protocol. Tells the browser to receive a website. Can be omitted from most browsers.

www = world wide web. Tells the browser the type of site, i. e. an unsecured freely available one.

bronxhistoricalsociety = the address.

.org, .com, .net, .gov, .edu, = these denote the type of license the website has.

bookstore = subdirectory, like a chapter in a book.

lifeinthebronx.html = web page.

The .html ending denotes hypertext mark up language. It is telling the browser what language to translate from (such as .xml, .html, .php).

Excellent Sites for Research on The Web Include:

www.bronxhistoricalsociety.org - The Bronx County Historical Society.

www.catnyp.nypl.org–Research Libraries of the New York Public Library.

www.loc.gov–Library of Congress.

www.smithsonian.org–The Smithsonian Institution.

www.co.westchester.ny.us/wcarchives–Westchester County Archives.

www.nytimes.com–*The New York Times*.

www.nysl.nysed,.gov–New York State Library.

www.radio-locator.com–A comprehensive radio station search engine, providing links to web pages and audio streams from radio stations in the United States and around the world.

www.imdb.com–The Internet Movie Database describes nearly every movie ever made in the United States.

www.chessclub.com–Internet Chess Club members play each other at various levels and speeds.

www.weather.com–Current weather and forecasts from anywhere in the world.

The Librarian

Please keep in mind that the Internet is as reliable as its sites and all material needs to be confirmed and rechecked. Do not rely on hearsay, blogs and chat room information.

While the "net" is an excellent tool for researchers it does not stop the need for library study. As of now, all library holdings are not digitized, and are not available on the web. So speak to a librarian when starting on your research journey as they are trained to be your guide to the collections.

The Teen Center of the new Bronx Library Center.
Courtesy of The New York Public Library.

10.

Suggestions for Improving Your Writing of History

1. Write in the past tense–history is in the past.
Using the past tense is always correct. This saves you
from getting into trouble with mixed tenses. "Napoleon
flees to Paris. Then the allies declined to exile him."
"Napoleon fled to Paris" would be best.

2. Write in the active voice, not in the passive–That
way the subject doesn't get lost and the verb is stronger.
"Ali flattened Foreman in the fifth" not "Foreman
was flattened in the fifth by Ali."

3. When you use a pronoun make sure that the
antecedent is absolutely clear. Is the particular he, she,
it, or they, that you use mean the only one your reader
can assume? "Alexander the Great kicked his horse.
He had a sore foot." So who had the sore foot? Don't be
afraid to repeat the subject by name to avoid confusion.

4. Make sure every sentence has a subject and a verb.

If you look out for these four problems and remedy them
you will have eliminated basic sources of confusion and
muddiness common to writing.

About Style

1. Don't try to put more than one idea into a sentence. For beginners, dependent clauses and the like tend to be a trap. Simplicity is always the answer.

2. Don't use a long word when a short one will do.

3. Is every word in your sentence necessary to make it clear? Get rid of anything that is not.

4. Does every sentence have a job to do in the paper? Does it present an idea, explain a concept, or give an example to prove the truth of your proposition?

5. Don't be vague when you can be specific. Don't write "the Americans thought…" when you mean "General Colin Powell of the Joint Chiefs of Staff thought." Learn to use examples.

6. Don't mix metaphors and avoid clichés (see George Orwell's essay "Politics and the English Language").

7. English is the language of Shakespeare and Poe. It is a beautiful instrument for expressing your ideas and has become the worldwide language. Treat it with respect. Use words carefully, paying close attention to their meaning. Keep a dictionary at your desk when you write. Learn to use a thesaurus and have one handy when you write as well.

With thanks to Prof. Frederick M. Binder.

The Adult Circulating and Reference Collections
on the third floor of The Bronx Library Center.
Courtesy of The New York Public Library.

Conclusion

The study and writing of history is a long
and enjoyable process.
The best work takes time and effort.
There are no short cuts to quality research writing.
Stick with it and you shall succeed.

Good luck.

Index

THE BRONX COUNTY HISTORICAL SOCIETY
Chartered in 1955.

Main Office: 3309 Bainbridge Avenue, The Bronx, NY 10467

The Bronx County Historical Society was founded for the purpose of promoting knowledge, interest and research in The Bronx and New York City. The Society administers The Museum of Bronx History, Edgar Allan Poe Cottage, a Research Library, and The Bronx County Archives; the founder of a new Bronx High School and The Bronx African-American History Project; publishes books, journals and newsletters; conducts school programs, historical tours, lectures, courses, archaeological digs and commemorations; designs exhibitions, sponsors various expeditions, and produces the Out of the Past radio show and cable television programs. The Society is active in furthering the arts, in preserving the natural resources of The Bronx, and in creating a sense of pride in the Bronx community.

MEMBERSHIP

Persons interested in historic studies, whether professionally or otherwise, are invited to membership.

Members of The Bronx County Historical Society receive:

Free admission to

MUSEUM OF BRONX HISTORY
3266 Bainbridge Avenue at East 208th Street, The Bronx, New York

and

EDGAR ALLAN POE COTTAGE
East Kingsbridge Road and Grand Concourse, The Bronx, New York

---

*50% discount on admission to member organizations
of the New York City History Coalition*

Invitation to
The Society's Annual High School Valedictorians Awards Program,
Bronx Authors Night, Historical Tours, Lectures, Exhibitions
and other Educational Projects

PUBLICATIONS AND SERVICES

The Bronx County Historical Society Journal is published two times a year and sent to all members. It is available by subscription to institutions.

The Society also publishes *The Bronx Historian* and *Library News*,
mailed to all members.

The Society produces a variety of books, pamphlets
and illustrated lectures and documentaries on historical subjects.
To promote history and assist historians, The Society offers many other
educational services, including an Institutional Services Program.

AWARDS AND BOOK PRIZES

William Beller Award–
for excellence and achievement on behalf of
The Bronx County Historical Society.

Poe Award of Literary Excellence–
dedicated to individuals who
have greatly contributed to the literary field.

John McNamara Trustees Award–
given to those people who espouse the positives
of New York.

Business Leader of the Year–
honoring those in business who support
the humanities and arts.

Carl M. and Nettie M. Halpern Memorial Award–
presented for the best reminiscence article published in
The Bronx County Historical Society Journal each year.

New York Urban History: Isabelle Hermalyn Book Award–
annual prize presented to the author of a
distinguished work in New York urban history.

Jonas Bronck Award–
presented to Bronxites who have contributed to
the best of society.

The Gouverneur Morris Visiting Scholars Program–
in honor of the Bronx Signer and Penman
of the United States Constitution.

Individuals, families, businesses or organizations interested in
becoming members and supporters of The Society may join by
contacting The Society by phone, e-mail or mail as indicated below.

CORRESPONDENCE

Inquiries should be addressed to:

THE BRONX COUNTY HISTORICAL SOCIETY

3309 Bainbridge Avenue, The Bronx, NY 10467.
Telephone: (718) 881-8900   Fax: (718) 881-4827
General e-mail address is: pderrick@bronxhistoricalsociety.org.
Our home page is: www.bronxhistoricalsociety.org.

PUBLICATIONS OF
THE BRONX COUNTY HISTORICAL SOCIETY

Life in The Bronx Series

The Birth of The Bronx: 1609-1900. (Lloyd Ultan & Gary Hermalyn)
The Bronx in the Innocent Years: 1890-1925. (Lloyd Ultan & Gary Hermalyn)
The Beautiful Bronx: 1920-1950. (Lloyd Ultan)
The Bronx It Was Only Yesterday: 1935-1965. (Lloyd Ultan & Gary Hermalyn)

The History of The Bronx Project

350th Anniversary of The Bronx Commemorative Issue.
    (Gary Hermalyn & Lloyd Ultan, Editors)
The Bronx in The Frontier Era: From The Beginning to 1696. (Lloyd Ultan)
Legacy of the Revolution: The Valentine-Varian House. (Lloyd Ultan)
Theatres of The Bronx. (Michael Miller)

The BCHS Journal

The Bronx County Historical Society Journal. (Peter Derrick, Editor)
25 Year Index to The Bronx County Historical Society Journal.
    (Gary Hermalyn, Editor)

New York City Series

Morris High School and the Creation of the New York City
    Public High School System. (Gary Hermalyn)
The Greater New York Centennial. (Elizabeth Beirne)
New York City at the Turn of the Century. (Elizabeth Beirne)
The Centennial of The Bronx Commemorative Issue.
    (Peter Derrick & Gary Hermalyn, Editors)
Tunneling To The Future. (Peter Derrick)

New York State Series

The Hudson River. (Elizabeth Beirne)

United States Series

Bicentennial of the United States Constitution Commemorative Issue.
    (Bro. Edward Quinn, Gary Hermalyn & Lloyd Ultan, Editors)

Roots of the Republic Series
(Dr. Gary Hermalyn, Project Editor)

Presidents of the United States. (Lloyd Ultan)
The First House of Representatives and The Bill of Rights. (George Lankevich)
The First Senate of The United States. (Richard Streb)
Chief Justices of The U.S. Supreme Court. (George Lankevich)
The Signers of the Constitution of the United States. (Bro. Edward Quinn)
The Signers of the Declaration of Independence. (Bro. Edward Quinn)

Research Library & Archives

The Bronx in Print. (Gary Hermalyn, Laura Tosi & Narcisco Rodriguez)
Elected Public Officials of The Bronx Since 1898.
  (Laura Tosi & Gary Hermalyn)
Genealogy of The Bronx. (Gary Hermalyn & Laura Tosi)
Publications of The Bronx County Historical Society Since 1955.
  (Gary Hermalyn)
Guide to The Bronx County Historical Society Media Collection.
  (Laura Tosi & Gary Hermalyn)
**Index to the Atlas Collection of The Bronx County Historical
  Society, 1868-1969.** (Laura Tosi & Gary Hermalyn)
Collections of The Bronx County Archives. (Dorthea Sartain & Peter Derrick)

Edgar Allan Poe Series

Poems and Tales of Edgar Allan Poe at Fordham. (Elizabeth Beirne)
Edgar Allan Poe Workbook. (Kathleen A. McAuley & Anthony C. Greene)

Streets of The City Series

**History in Asphalt: The Origin of Bronx Street &
  Place Names Encyclopedia.** (John McNamara)
McNamara's Old Bronx. (John McNamara)
History of Morris Park Racecourse. (Nicholas DiBrino)
Landmarks of The Bronx. (Gary Hermalyn & Robert Kornfeld)
Bronx Views: Post Cards of The Bronx. (Gary Hermalyn & Thomas X. Casey)

Educational Material

The South Bronx and the Founding of America. (Lisa Garrison)
Latin Bicentennial. (Alfonso Serrano)
West Farms Local History Curriculum Guide. (Samuel Hopkins)
Local History Classroom Resource Guide. (Dan Eisenstein)
The Study and Writing of History. (Gary Hermalyn)
Annotated Primary Source Documents. (Anthony C. Greene)

Of Special Interest

The Bronx Cookbook. (Peter Derrick & Gary Hermalyn, Editors)

---

*For a complete list of Videotapes and Radio Show Cassettes
or to order Books, or for a copy of our catalogue
of Books and Gifts, please write or call:*

THE BRONX COUNTY HISTORICAL SOCIETY

3309 Bainbridge Avenue, The Bronx, New York 10467
(718) 881-9900   Fax: (718) 881-4827
Visit our website www.bronxhistoricalsociety.org

EDGAR ALLAN POE COTTAGE
c. 1812

Edgar Allan Poe spent the last years of his life, from
1846 to 1849, in The Bronx at Poe Cottage. Administered
by The Society since 1975, the landmark Poe Cottage, built in 1812,
has period furnishings and is open for guided tours.

• Poe Park–Grand Concourse and East Kingsbridge Road, The Bronx •

MUSEUM OF BRONX HISTORY
c. 1758

The Valentine-Varian House, built in 1758, in pre-revolutionary
times by Isaac Valentine, was donated to The Society
in 1965. Today, the restored house is open to the
public to enjoy its many exhibits of Bronx history.

• 3309 Bainbridge Avenue, The Bronx •

For further information about these historic sites,
the Society's Research Library, the Bronx Archives,
and our educational programs, please visit our website–
www.bronxhistoricalsociety.org or call 718-881-8900.

*The Bronx County Historical Society is supported
in part with public funds and services provided through
The Department of Cultural Affairs and
The Department of Parks and Recreation of the City of New York,
The City Council Delegation of The Bronx,
The Office of The Bronx Borough President,
The Bronx Delegations of the NYS Assembly and NYS Senate,
Historic House Trust of New York City,
The New York State Office of Parks, Recreation
and Historic Preservation,
and The New York State Library.*

Dr. Gary Hermalyn

GARY HERMALYN is C.E.O. of The Bronx County Historical Society and president of the History of New York City Project Inc. Historian, educator, lecturer, and publisher, he earned a doctorate from Columbia University.

Dr. Hermalyn is the project editor of *The United States Supreme Court,* a ten-volume series and the six-volume *Roots of The Republic,* author of *Morris High School and The Creation of The New York City Public High School System, Time and The Calendar* a book and planetarium program, and the co-author of the four-volume *Life in The Bronx* book series.

Editor/publisher of 125 publications including *American Metropolis: A History of NYC; History in Asphalt: The Origin of Bronx Street and Place Names Encyclopedia; The Hudson River; The Signers of the Declaration of Independence; The Greater New York Centennial;* and *Poems & Tales of Edgar Allan Poe at Fordham.*

Dr. Hermalyn is an associate editor of the *Encyclopedia of New York City* and is a Centennial Historian of New York City.